The Clever Teens' Tales
From World War Two

Felix Rhodes

Complete Series:

Contents

The Clever Teens' Tales
From World War Two

31 August 1939,
World War Two's First Death

World War Two began with a single death; a death that Hitler would use as the justification for going to war and invading Poland. The victim's name, largely forgotten to history, was Franciszek (or Franz) Honiok.

Eastward ambition

The signing of the Nazi-Soviet Non-Aggression Pact on 23 August 1939, had been the penultimate piece in Hitler's grand jigsaw. With the Soviet Union safely out of the way, Hitler was now free to pursue his ambitions in the West.

Three days later, on 26 August, Hitler ordered the invasion of Poland. Troops had begun to mobilize only for Hitler, nervous of Britain's response, to rescind the order. He knew he couldn't simply march in – he needed a pretext. In the event he made one up.

On 28 August, Hitler revoked the German-Polish Non-Aggression Treaty of 1934. The Poles knew what was coming.

On the nights leading up to 31 August / 1 September there were no less than twenty-one incidences along the German – Polish border faked by the Germans which, to a gullible world, would seem like acts of Polish aggression for which retaliation was perfectly justifiable.

Operation Himmler

These acts of farce, codenamed Operation Himmler, were organised by Heinrich Himmler and Reinhard Heydrich. The most notorious was the Gleiwitz Incident, the faked attack on the radio transmitting station, a few miles inside Germany, near the border town of Gleiwitz in the Silesia region. Early evening on 31 August 1939, SS soldiers, dressed up as Polish partisans and led by a notorious Nazi thug, Major Alfred Naujocks, 'attacked' the German transmitter and its German guards (more SS men dressed up), and broadcast in Polish a brief anti-German message.

To make the attack look more authentic, the Germans had brought along an inmate from the Dachau concentration camp, the forty-three-year-old Franciszek Honiok (pictured above), a farmer and a known Polish sympathizer, arrested by the Gestapo just the day before. The unfortunate Honiok was, what the Germans called, 'canned goods', kept alive until the Gestapo had need for a dead but still warm body.

Having dressed Honiok as a Polish bandit, they drugged him unconscious, shot him at the scene and then left his body there as evidence of the supposed attack. Local police and press found the body and the news spread across Europe. 'There have been reports of an attack on a radio station in Gleiwitz,' reported the BBC. 'Several of the Poles were reported killed, but the numbers are not yet known.' The attack made the *New York Times* the following day.

Hitler knew that the falsehood of Operation Himmler was highly transparent but, as he lectured his staff the week before, 'I need a propagandistic cause for declaring war, whether convincing or not. The victor will not be asked whether he told the truth'.

4.45 a.m. World War Two starts

The following morning, 1 September, at 4.45 German troops attacked Poland. Hours later Hitler spoke to the nation, referring to the 'Polish atrocities'. He continued,

3

'This night for the first time Polish regular soldiers fired on our own territory. This group of Polish Army hooligans has finally exhausted our patience. Since 5.45 a. m. we have been returning the fire… I will continue this struggle, no matter against whom, until the safety of the Reich and its rights are secured.' Whether by accident or design, Hitler was an hour out.

Rudolph Hess, getting carried away in hyperbole, declared, 'There is bloodshed, Herr Chamberlain! There are dead! Innocent people have died. The responsibility for this, however, lives with England, which talks of peace while fanning the flames of war. England that has point blank refused all the Fuhrer's proposals for peace throughout the years.'

Technically, Franciszek Honiok had been killed during peacetime but his death can be considered the first in a conflict that would, over the ensuing six years, claim over fifty million victims.

The Second World War had begun.

May 1940
The evacuation of Dunkirk

On 10 May 1940, Germany launched their attack against France and the Low Countries.

We have the Maginot Line

There was much disquiet amongst Hitler's generals; they considered his plan of attack as reckless. Equally, amongst the French, was a firm belief that France would not fall. For one thing – the French had the Maginot Line. This defensive 280 mile long fortification, that ran along the Franco-German border, was built in the early thirties precisely for this purpose – to keep out the Germans.

The Germans rendered it obsolete within a morning

The Germans came through the Ardennes forest, which, because of its rugged terrain, the French considered impassable, then merely skirted round the north of the Maginot Line, reaching the town of Sedan on the French side of the Ardennes on 14 May. Brushing aside French resistance, the Germans pushed, not towards Paris as expected, but north, across the Verdun, towards the English Channel, forcing the French and British troops further and further back.

In 1916, despite ten months of intensive trench warfare, the Germans had failed to take Verdun. In May 1940, it took them one day.

The situation was getting worse by the day. Rotterdam was heavily bombed and, on 15 May, the Dutch, fearing further losses, capitulated. On 28 May Belgium also surrendered.

Trapped

In northern France the Germans took Boulogne, then Calais. By the end of May, with their backs to the sea, over a third of a million Allied troops were trapped in the French coastal town of Dunkirk subject to German shells and attacks from the air. It was only a matter of days before the full-blown assault would come.

But the Germans, poised to annihilate the whole British Expeditionary Force, were inexplicably ordered by Hitler to halt outside the town.

Meanwhile, from within Dover, the British pressed into service every military vessel it could lay its hands on. The evacuation started but it wasn't anywhere near enough.

Panic

With the aerial assault shredding nerves, Dunkirk witnessed scenes of panic as fear and the sense of entrapment caused discipline to break. Men fought for space on the ships and boats, often capsizing the very vessels that had come to rescue them. Officers shot their men for losing self-control. Knowing that they were trapped, ready to be plucked off at any moment, is a feeling that cannot be imagined.

The men in Dover, realising Hitler could finish the situation off at any moment of his choosing, gathered every civilian vessel, large or small, that could float, the 'little ships', and sent them across the Channel.

Losses were heavy but by 4 June the evacuation had brought back to Britain 338,226 British, French, and other Allied soldiers. Plus 170 dogs. Soldiers put much store by their mascots. Meanwhile, Hitler's generals watched, puzzled and ruing an opportunity missed.

A deliverance

On 4 June, in the House of Commons, British Prime Minister, Winston Churchill, was careful not to call the 'miracle of Dunkirk' a victory but merely a 'deliverance'. He continued to deliver his famous "We shall fight on the beaches" speech, concluding with the immortal words, "We shall never surrender."

The French, however, saw it somewhat differently – with the Germans closing in on Paris, they considered the evacuation of Dunkirk not in terms of an heroic rescue, but as a huge betrayal. The British had betrayed them.

On 22 June, France surrendered to the Germans.

Charles de Gaulle's Appeal of 18 June 1940

Charles de Gaulle's *L'Appel du 18 Juin*, the 'Appeal of 18 June', is of huge symbolic importance for the French. Former French president, Nicolas Sarkozy, once said "We (the French) are all children of the 18 June".

On 14 June 1940, Hitler's forces entered Paris, a city largely deserted with over two million Parisians having fled south to escape the Nazi invasion.

Charles de Gaulle

De Gaulle had fought with great distinction during the First World War and was thrice wounded. At the Battle of Verdun he served under Philippe Pétain, whom he greatly admired and who was to become his mentor. During the Battle of Verdun, on 2 March 1916, de Gaulle was taken prisoner by the Germans. He tried unsuccessfully to escape five times and was only released following the armistice in November 1918.

Charles de Gaulle, c1942. Library of Congress.

Following the Great War, de Gaulle served in Poland, Germany and the Middle East. He became convinced that future wars should rely on tanks and aircraft, thus avoiding the static stalemate of the previous war. The same conclusion had been reached in Germany but while, from 1939 the Germans acted on it, the French did not, putting far too much faith in the Maginot Line, France's fortified line of defence along the Franco-German border built during the 1930s. Indeed, de Gaulle's belief in mobile warfare, which he espoused in a number of books, won him many enemies within the French high command, not least from his old friend, Pétain, and may have been the cause for the lack of further promotion within the army.

Leader of all free Frenchmen

With the German invasion of France in 1940, de Gaulle, in command of a tank division, put up a gallant defence but, outnumbered, finally succumbed. France's French prime minister, Paul Reynaud, appointed de Gaulle to the ministry of war, thus de Gaulle's military career abruptly gave way to politics.

On 15 June, de Gaulle, was whisked out of France on an aeroplane sent by Winston Churchill to begin his life of exile in London. At the age of forty-nine, De Gaulle was the youngest and most junior general in the French Army and had only been a government minister for two weeks. Although he had fought at Dunkirk and had met Churchill he was generally unknown. French people certainly hadn't heard of him and had no idea what he looked like.

When de Gaulle first arrived in London, Churchill asked a colleague, 'Why have you brought this lanky, gloomy brigadier?' The man replied: 'Because no one else would come.'

In London de Gaulle sought permission to broadcast to France from the studios of the BBC. The British cabinet refused, not wanting to upset the new regime freshly installed in France. Churchill, however, stepped in and granted the Frenchman his wish.

I speak for France

And so, on 18 June 1940, Charles de Gaulle was led to Studio 4B in the BBC's broadcasting House and there met BBC producer, Elizabeth Barker. (Barker was one of the very few women to hold the role of producer. She was later reprimanded for meeting her illustrious French guest while not wearing stockings). In a 'very deep, resonant voice', according to Barker, De Gaulle broadcast his declaration, asserting that France was not alone, "*La France n'est pas seule!*" "The flame of the French resistance," he cried, "must not be extinguished and will not be extinguished". (The same day, Church delivered his iconic 'This was their finest hour' speech to the House of Commons).

At the time, very few heard the general's auspicious words. Although, another future French president, Giscard d'Estaing, did hear the broadcast: 'We heard that a French general would speak and we listened to him with no idea who he was. It had a huge effect on us all. We all understood that the war was not lost... The appeal said the war is not over.'

De Gaulle returned the following day and this unknown Frenchman with his patriotic-sounding name boldly announced, "I, General de Gaulle, a French soldier and military leader, realise that I now speak for France." That month alone, June 1940, he broadcast eight times.

Surrender

The BBC however had failed to record De Gaulle's initial speeches and the general insisted on doing them again – for the sake of prosperity. He waited until the French had formally surrendered, which they did on 22 June – in a railway carriage, the same railway carriage fifty miles northeast of Paris that the Germans had surrendered to the French in 1918.

This time, on 22 June, the microphones were on and De Gaulle re-read and recorded the *L'Appel du 18 Juin*. His words soon spread and became the battle cry of the Free French movement.

The new French government was led by the eighty-four-year-old Marshal Philippe Petain (pictured below on 24 October 1940 shaking hands with Hitler), hero of the 1916 Battle of Verdun. Petain accepted France's defeat and immediately his puppet government was enforcing Nazi rule from the spa town of Vichy in central France. One of its first acts was to sentence De Gaulle to death – in *absentia*. Indeed, on 17 June Petain delivered his own speech in which he said, 'we are defeated and will accept an armistice'.

De Gaulle became the self-appointed leader of the 'Free French'. In May 1943, he moved to Algiers, a French colony, and there established the French Committee for National Liberation, with himself as its president. A year later, the ever-confident de Gaulle renamed the FCNL the

Provisional Government of the French Republic.

Man of destiny

Winston Churchill considered de Gaulle as a 'man of destiny' but their relationship was never an easy one. De Gaulle's relationship with US president, Franklin D Roosevelt, was even worse. Roosevelt was furious that de Gaulle should take it upon himself to assume the role of president of a provisional government, and refused to acknowledge de Gaulle's self-appointed political title.

Roosevelt had instructed Churchill to exclude de Gaulle from having any input into the planned Allied invasion of France. On the eve of the invasion in June 1944, however, Churchill decided that de Gaulle had to be informed. On 4 June, de Gaulle was in Algiers and Churchill sent a plane to bring him back to London. At first, de Gaulle refused to return until, with a bit of arm-twisting, he was persuaded. De Gaulle had been angered by Roosevelt's insistence that come liberation, he planned to install, not a provisional government headed by de Gaulle, but a provisional Allied military government. When Churchill urged de Gaulle to seek a rapprochement with Roosevelt, de Gaulle responded angrily, 'Why should I lodge my candidacy for power in France with Roosevelt? The French government already exists.'

De Gaulle's fear was that if he didn't act fast enough, the French communists, who had also been active within the resistance, would seize power come liberation.

In London, de Gaulle was asked to broadcast a message to the Free French. But on reading Eisenhower's planned speech, due to be delivered before his, de Gaulle was furious that the American had made no mention of him or the Free French. Finally, however, de Gaulle made his speech.

De Gaulle wanted to return to France at the first possible opportunity. Churchill refused permission until a week after D-Day. On 14 June, almost four years to the day since leaving, de Gaulle stepped foot on French soil, and, visiting the recently-liberated town of Bayeux, was greeted with much enthusiasm.

Paris liberated!

Two months later, on 25 August, Paris was liberated. The following day, de Gaulle made his triumphant return. In his speech, he proclaimed, 'Paris outraged, Paris broken, Paris martyred, but Paris liberated! By herself, liberated by her people, with the help of the whole of France!' His administration was officially recognised by the Allies but de Gaulle was deeply offended that France was still not considered one of the Great Powers or invited to the 'Big Three' conferences with Churchill, Roosevelt and Stalin at Yalta and Potsdam.

On 15 August 1945, Pétain was tried for his collaboration with the Nazis and found guilty. The eighty-nine-year-old Marshal was sentenced to death by firing squad. De Gaulle however stepped in and taking into account Pétain's age and his First World War record, commuted Pétain's death sentence to life imprisonment. (Pétain was imprisoned, in relative luxury, on the island of Île d'Yeu, on the Atlantic coast of France. Increasingly frail, he needed constant care. He died on 23 July 1951, aged ninety-five.)

On 10 September 1944, the Provisional Government of the French Republic was formed. At its head as prime minister – Charles de Gaulle. A year later, on 13 November 1945, following elections, de Gaulle was confirmed in his post as provisional head. However, he didn't last long. Disillusioned with coalition politics, de Gaulle resigned in January 1946.

France is a widow

In 1947, he formed his own party, the right-wing Rally of the French People (RFP) but, failing to gain support, de Gaulle resigned in 1951. The party disbanded in 1953.

Returning to politics in 1958, after seven years of retirement, de Gaulle was again elected president. This time, he remained in power for ten years during which time he granted independence to all thirteen of France's colonies, most notably Algeria following the seven-year Algerian War; survived several assassination attempts;

advanced France's atomic capabilities; and negotiated France's inclusion into the European Economic Community, and its removal from NATO. He survived the political turmoil caused by the student riots during 1968, and resigned in April 1969.

He didn't have long to enjoy his second retirement. Charles de Gaulle died of a heart attack on 9 November 1970, two weeks short of his eightieth birthday. Upon his death, Georges Pompidou, the president, announced his predecessor's death with the words, 'General de Gaulle is dead. France is a widow.'

22 June 1940
France Surrenders

On 11 November 1918, the French and British allies accepted Germany's surrender and, between them, signed the armistice that ended the First World War. The signing took place in a railway carriage in the middle of the picturesque woods of Compiègne, fifty miles north-east of Paris. The humiliation of that event ran deep into the psyche of Germany, and none more so than in Adolf Hitler, at the time a corporal in the Imperial German Army.

On 22 June 1940, Hitler, now the German *Führer*, got his revenge – it was the turn of the French to surrender, and Hitler made sure that it was done in the most demeaning circumstances possible – in exactly the same train carriage and in the same spot as the signing twenty-two years earlier.

German soldiers in Paris, June 1940. German Federal Archive.

The swastika flies over Paris

The fall of France was dramatic in its speed. German Chief of General Staff, Franz Halder, who had organised the invasion of Poland eight months earlier, warned Hitler of the folly of attacking France. Privately, he believed it to be 'idiotic and reckless'. In the event, Hitler's forces entered a largely deserted Paris on 14 June, over two million Parisians having fled south. Soon the swastika flag was flying from the Arc de Triomphe.

On 16 June, the French general, Charles de Gaulle, escaped France to begin his life of exile in London.

In Britain, Winston Churchill, appointed prime minister only on 10 May, urged the French to keep on fighting and discussed the possibility of France and Great Britain becoming one unified nation. When French prime minister, Paul Reynaud, put the idea of the union to the French government, now based in Bordeaux, the idea was ridiculed. Marshal Philippe Pétain, hero of the 1916 Battle of Verdun, preferred to surrender – to continue the fight would destroy the country and a union with Britain would be akin to a 'marriage with a corpse'. French general, Maxime Weygand, believed that following the fall of France, the British would soon have 'its neck wrung like a chicken' by the Germans.

On 17 June, Reynaud resigned, to be replaced by the eighty-four-year-old Pétain, whose first acts were to seek an armistice with the Germans and order Reynaud's arrest. France had been defeated.

The Forest of Compiègne

On 20 June, the Germans prepared the text for the French-German armistice, with Hitler dictating its preamble. The venue for the signing was to be the forest of Compiègne, where, twenty-two years before, at the end of the First World War, the Germans had surrendered to the French and signed the armistice of 11 November 1918. Hitler, with a flair for the dramatic, ordered that the signing ceremony should take place in the in the very same railway carriage that had been used in November 1918, now on display in a Parisian museum. The carriage, once a dining car which had been transformed into a conference room, split into two by a glass partition, was transported north.

Weeping Frenchman.
National Archives and Records Administration.

About two hundred yards from the carriage stood the Alsace-Lorraine statue, commemorating the 1918 signing, featuring a fallen German eagle, impaled by the sword of the victorious allies. Now, in June 1940, it was adorned by the Nazi swastika. Nearby stood a statue of Marshal Ferdinand Foch, the French commander-in-chief, who had led the negotiations in 1918.

At three fifteen on the afternoon of 21 June, a warm summer's day, the German delegation arrived and emerged from their Mercedes: Hermann Goring, Rudolph Hess, Joachim von Ribbentrop, Wilhelm Keitel, Erich Raeder, Alfred Jodl amongst others and, last of all, Hitler, his First World War Iron Cross pinned upon his tunic.

The American journalist and writer, William Shirer, author of the excellent, *Rise and Fall of the Third Reich*, originally published 1959, was witness to the occasion.

Shirer describes the expression in Hitler's face: 'grave, solemn, yet brimming with revenge... There was something else, difficult to describe, in his expression, a sort of scornful, inner joy at being present at this great reversal he himself had wrought.'

Hitler and his entourage stopped to read the French inscription of a granite block, which read in capitals, 'HERE ON THE ELEVENTH OF NOVEMBER 1918 SUCCUMBED THE CRIMINAL PRIDE OF THE GERMAN EMPIRE – VANQUISHED BY THE FREE PEOPLES WHICH IT TRIED TO ENSLAVE.'

The German delegation took their place in the carriage, Hitler pointedly sitting where Foch had sat twenty-two years before. Then arrived the French delegation, headed by General Charles Huntziger. Shirer noticed that the German guard of honour, 'snapped to attention for the French as they passed but did not present arms'.

With everyone sitting, Keitel, with a monocle in his eye, read aloud Hitler's preamble of the armistice, a translator relaying it to the French. At the glass partition, one of Hitler's henchmen, Otto Günsche (who took on the responsibility of burning Hitler's body following his leader's suicide on 30 April 1945), kept guard with orders to shoot anyone who 'should dare to conduct himself in an improper manner towards Hitler'.

Hitler uttered not a word. With the reading of the preamble done, Hitler and most of his entourage made their exit with a Nazi salute, and left to the sound of the German national anthem and the *Horst Wessel* song (a Nazi favourite composed in memory of a Nazi 'martyr') ringing in their ears. The French delegates stood, some with tears in their eyes.

The French sign the Armistice

Keitel and Jodl stayed behind to discuss the details of the armistice with Huntziger. France was to be split into two – the northern half occupied by the Germans and the southern half run by a French government answerable to the Germans. This government, headed by Pétain, was to be based in the spa town of Vichy.

At 18:30, the following day, with the Germans getting impatient, the French were given one hour to sign or face a resumption of hostilities. Huntziger, speaking to General Weygand in Bordeaux, insisted that he should be *ordered* to sign the armistice and not merely *authorized* to sign it, thereby removing the responsibility from his shoulders. At 18:50, Huntziger and Keitel duly signed the hateful document.

On hearing the news, Hitler was thrilled, slapping his knee with delight. (Exactly one year later, he would launch the German invasion of the Soviet Union.)

Straight afterwards, on Hitler's orders, the railway carriage and the monument commemorating the 1918 signing were destroyed. The following day, Hitler enjoyed a three-hour whistle-stop tour of Paris. Having taken in the main sites and been photographed with the Eiffel Tower behind him, he left. It was, he said, 'the dream of my life to be permitted to see Paris. I cannot say how happy I am to have that dream fulfilled today.' On visiting Napoleon's tomb, he said: 'That was the greatest and finest moment of my life'. Before departing, he ordered the demolition of two Parisian First World War monuments, including the monument to Edith Cavell, the British nurse shot by the Germans in Brussels in October 1915.

The German occupation of France would last four long years until in August 1944, two months from the start of the Normandy landings, the first parts of France were finally liberated.

30 June 1940
The German Occupation of the
Channel Islands

There was, at the start of the Second World War, a small British garrison stationed on the Channel Islands but Churchill decided that the Islands could not be defended and were to be demilitarised.

Of the pre-war population of 96,000, a quarter were evacuated to Britain. On 21 June 1940, the last British soldiers also departed and, in doing so, left the remaining islanders to their fate. The Germans, unaware of this and that the Islands were there for the taking, bombed the Guernsey and Jersey harbours on 28 June, killing forty-four civilians. Two days later, on 30 June, the island of Guernsey surrendered, swiftly followed by Jersey, Alderney and Sark.

The only part of Great Britain to be occupied by the Germans throughout the war, the islands were not of any strategic importance for the Germans beyond denying the British the option of using them as a base. Also, occupation of British territory was symbolically important to the Germans. In the early years the islands were used as a holiday destination for German troops serving in France.

The Nazis take control

Immediately the occupiers established control and stamped their authority. It was often the seemingly inconsequential things that irked the most: the changing of the time to fit in with German time; changing which side of the road to drive on. But as most cars were requisitioned by the Germans and fuel was heavily rationed, it made little difference and horse-drawn traffic was soon a regular sight on the Guernsey roads.

Using forced labour imported from across occupied Europe, the Germans fortified the islands and built an underground hospital for their troops wounded in France. Four concentration camps were also built on Alderney, an island which had largely been evacuated before the invasion. One of the Alderney camps was specifically for Jews, and islanders who had had just one Jewish grandparent were deemed Jewish and were therefore especially vulnerable. British police officers in British police uniforms were used to arrest the Islands' Jews.

Concentration camps on British soil

The camps, the only concentration camps on British soil, opened in January 1942 and, with a capacity of about 6,000, held prisoners from all over Europe. They were designed to house forced labourers rather than exterminate but, nevertheless, the camps saw the death of over 700 inmates during the two years of their existence. The camps were closed in 1944 and the survivors transported to Germany. For many the death camps awaited.

The islanders had received orders from London not to resist but the intensity of occupation, with almost one German for every two islanders, rendered active resistance virtually impossible anyway. But individual acts of defiance and heroism were common. The most daring examples were islanders who hid those in danger of internment.

British citizens deported

In 1942, as a reprisal for German civilians taken by the British in Iran, Hitler decreed that citizens not born on the islands were to be deported to camps in Germany. Some 2,000 British citizens were deported, many never to return.

The supply of food and fuel from Germany through France, although rationed, had not been a severe problem until the Allied Normandy Invasion in June 1944. Once the Allies had secured northern France, supplies to the islands came to an abrupt halt. Churchill considered opinion of the situation was to "let them rot". Both occupier and occupied starved and it wasn't for another six months, in December 1944, that the first International Red Cross ship arrived with much-needed supplies.

Our dear Channel Islands

On 8 May, the war in Europe ended. Broadcasting from London, Churchill announced the "unconditional surrender of all German land, sea and air forces in Europe." He added, "And I should not forget to mention that our dear Channel Islands, the only part of His Majesty's Dominions that has been in the hands of the German foe, are also to be freed today."

The German occupiers of the Channel Islands surrendered unconditionally and, early in the morning 9 May, the first ships bearing the Islanders' liberators docked.

Immediately the celebrations began: processions, parties, speeches, prayers, the singing of the National Anthem and the raising of the Union Jack. But also the reprisals began: women who had fraternised with the Germans, 'Jerry Bags', were particularly vulnerable to swift justice. Known collaborators and informants were also targeted. Accusations of collaboration were investigated with the view to prosecution but none came to court.

On 7 June, King George and Queen Elizabeth visited the islands. By the end of 1945 all those evacuated off the islands during the spring of 1940 had returned home.

Total collaboration

And there ends the tale of stoical resistance and British stubbornness and pride. But beneath it all lurks the unsavoury taint of collaboration: "the Channel Islands' war history was one of almost total collaboration with the Nazis," wrote Julia Pascal, author of *Theresa*, a play about wartime Guernsey. Pascal, writing in *The Guardian* in September 2002, goes on to say, "Many on Guernsey believe that the Channel Islands government willingly served their Nazi masters... The occupation has been bleached out of British history."

But the Islanders of today still celebrate Liberation Day each year.

14 November 1940
The Coventry Blitz

A beautiful medieval city, Coventry had developed during the century before the Second World War into a major industrial city and leading manufacturer of munitions. But on the night of 14/15 November 1940 it was almost "wiped off the map".

The Battle of Britain

The Battle of Britain had been raging above the skies of South England throughout the summer of 1940 and, in more recent weeks, the German Luftwaffe had begun bombing areas of population. The Blitz had begun.

London, Birmingham, Plymouth, Sheffield, Glasgow and other cities had all become victim to Hitler's attempt to destroy the fabric of British urban life and demoralise its population. Now it was Coventry's turn. But unlike the other cities, Coventry was comparatively small – the destruction wrought was far greater in relative terms.

"Women were seen to cry," wrote the Mass Observation report, "to scream, to tremble all over, to faint in the street, to attack a fireman, and so on…"

Fire!

In an operation codenamed Moonlight Sonata, wave after wave of German bombers dropped high explosive and incendiary bombs over the city centre and throughout the city. Hitler, it was said, had ordered the raid as revenge for an RAF attack on Munich.

The immediate destruction hampered the work of the fire engines and ambulances as craters and falling rubble and debris made access almost impossible. Ambulances arriving from Birmingham fared no better. The water mains had been hit, restricting the supply of water and, to add to the chaos, the fire brigade's HQ had taken a direct hit.

The city's anti-aircraft guns made little impact. The Germans lost only one plane, and that was from a 'mysterious' crash. One Luftwaffe pilot, dropping bombs from 6,000 feet, felt his nostrils 'prickling – I could smell the city burning'. Between raids, the German planes returned to French bases to load more bombs. Five hundred tons of high explosive bombs, and 30,000 incendiaries were dropped.

One witness on the ground spoke of 'people staggering about in shock, as though they were hopelessly drunk. Some, so frightened, were bordering on madness.' Soon there were 'large open spaces where, a little while ago, there had been blocks of buildings.' Another described the 'surreal scenes: hundreds of dogs and cats turned into strays overnight; a man boiling a kettle on an incendiary bomb'.

Another, witnessing the destruction of a dairy, remembered having 'to run for my life from a knee-high river of boiling butter... I saw a whole pig roasting in a butcher's window'.

The All-Clear

After eleven hours of sustained bombing the German planes drifted away as dawn rose. Finally at 6.15 a.m. the all-clear was sounded. Hardly a single building in the city centre remained standing. 60,000 out of 75,000 buildings had been hit and damaged, including 111 factories. The city had been laid waste, left smouldering in the early morning rain. The ancient Coventry cathedral of St Michael's had been hit several times and incendiaries had caused a firestorm within, although its spire remained in tact. On visiting the city and viewing the destruction, King George VI is said to have wept on seeing the ruins of the burnt-out cathedral.

Winston Churchill visiting Coventry in September 1941.

The official death toll numbered 568, most too badly burnt to be identified, but such was the intensity of fire that the real figure was likely to have been considerably more. About 420 were buried in a mass grave. Thousands more were injured.

Two days later, on 16 November, Britain retaliated, the RAF bombing the German city of Hamburg, killing

233 civilians. Meanwhile, the *Birmingham Gazette* exclaimed, 'Coventry – Our Guernica', in reference to the German bombing of the Basque town on 26 April 1937 during the Spanish Civil War.

To Coventrate

Hitler's Minister for Propaganda, Joseph Goebbels, invented a new verb to describe the virtual destruction of a city during war – to 'Coventrate'.

Coventry fell victim again – in April 1941 and August 1942 but it was the devastation of this night, in November 1940, that came to symbolise the terror of the Blitz.

German cities suffered in even greater measure – for every ton of bomb that fell on British cities during the early part of the war, three hundred fell on German cities

Sixteen years later, in 1956, Coventry and Dresden were twinned.

24 May 1941
The Sinking of HMS *Hood*

On 24 May 1941 two mighty ships engaged in battle – the respective pride of the German and British navies: the *Bismarck* and HMS *Hood*.

It started six days before when, on the evening of Sunday 18 May 1941, the *Bismarck*, accompanied by the *Prinz Eugene*, set sail from the Polish port of Gdynia. It was the *Bismarck's* first mission.

There had never been a warship like her

Named after the 19th century German chancellor, Otto von Bismarck, the *Bismarck* had been launched just two years earlier, in February 1939, by the chancellor's great granddaughter. The ship was an impressive sight – one sixth of a mile long and 120 feet wide. British writer and broadcaster, Ludovic Kennedy (1909-2009), wrote of the *Bismarck*: 'There had never been a warship like her... No German saw her without pride, no neutral or enemy without admiration.'

The mission set for the *Bismarck* and the *Prinz Eugene* was to head for the Atlantic and cause as much damage and disruption as possible to the British convoys shipping vital supplies across the Atlantic into Britain. On board the *Bismarck* were two of Hitler's most senior and able seamen – its captain, forty-five-year-old Ernst Lindemann, referred to by his crew as 'our father', and Fleet Commander, fifty-one-year-old Admiral Gunther Lutjens.

From Poland, the two ships passed Norway where their presence was picked up by the British. British aircraft and ships, keeping a safe distance, monitored their progress as the German ships skirted north of Iceland and then south down the Denmark Straits between Iceland and Greenland.

It was here, in the Denmark Straits, that the British fleet, led by HMS *Hood* and *Prince of Wales*, was ordered to intercept.

The embodiment of British sea-power

Built in 1916, the *Hood* was, according to Kennedy, 'the embodiment of British sea-power and the British Empire between the wars.' But the *Hood* had been built at a time, during the First World War, when enemy shells came in low and hit the sides of a ship near the water line. But in 1941 shells were more likely to arch across the sky and fall onto the upper decks. The decks of the *Hood* had never been reinforced and therein lay its weak spot. The 'embodiment of British sea-power' had been built for a different war.

Painting by J.C. Schmitz-Westerholt capturing the moment of the Hood's *sinking.*

The Battle of Denmark Straits

In the early hours of 24 May, the opposing fleets with their imposing ships engaged. Thirteen miles apart the ships fired one-ton shells that, travelling at 1,600 miles per hour, took almost a minute to reach their intended target. The noise, which could be heard in Iceland, was horrendous.

The battle lasted merely twenty minutes and both the *Bismarck* and the *Prince of Wales* took direct hits, but it was the fate of the *Hood* that stunned the world. A shell from the *Bismarck* hit the *Hood* on its vulnerable upper deck, tore through the ship and penetrated its ammunition room, causing an almighty explosion.

The ship sliced into two, its front end dramatically lifting out of the water. A huge fireball rocketed into the sky, followed by plumes of dense black smoke, with pieces of molten metal shooting like so many white stars, as one German sailor described it.

Within five minutes, the HMS *Hood*, pride of the Royal Navy, had sunk. It was no more. Of its crew of 1,421 men, all were killed – except for three.

The crew of the *Bismarck* was jubilant. For this they would be the toast of Germany. The *Prince of Wales* was also struggling, having been hit seven times. The German crew wanted to give chase and finish her off but Lindemann, as captain, not wanting to expose the *Bismarck* unnecessarily, erred on the side of caution and resisted the temptation.

Also, of greater concern for Lindemann, the *Bismarck* had been hit by a shell that failed to explode but had caused damage to her fuel tanks. Serious damage.

Leaking oil at an alarming rate, Lindemann knew he had to get her back to safety. He decided on Saint-Nazaire, northern France, a distance of 1,700 miles, a journey of some four days.

The *Prinz Eugene* and the *Bismarck* parted ways. The joy of the *Bismarck* crew had evaporated. Now there was nothing but concern – could they escape the British, could they make it all the way to France? The ship was limping – the fuel leak had forced the captain to greatly reduce speed. France seemed a long way away.

Sink the *Bismarck*

Meanwhile, in Britain, a nation reeled in shock, stunned by the loss of the *Hood*. It demanded retaliation. Churchill, reflecting the public mood, issued his famous battle cry: 'Sink the *Bismarck!*'

A fleet consisting of four battleships, two battle cruisers, two aircraft carriers, twenty-one destroyers and thirteen cruisers was dispatched.

The chase was on.

27 May 1941
Sink the Bismarck

On 24 May 1941, the *Bismarck*, on its first operation, had helped sink the HMS *Hood*. But in return, it had been damaged and had set a course for northern France to attend to its wounds and repair the leaking fuel tanks. "The *Hood* was the pride of England," said the German Fleet Commander, Admiral Günter Lutjens, over the ship's loudspeakers, "the enemy will now attempt to concentrate his forces against us. The German nation is with you."

The crew was nervous but for now at least the ship had slipped away from battle and had managed to remain at large, undetected by the British.

But then Lutjens made a fatal error – he broke radio silence. He radioed back to Germany announcing his intentions. The signal was picked up by the British, and the codebreakers at Bletchley Park did their work and roughly located the *Bismarck*'s position. Then, a RAF reconnaissance plane spotted the trailing oil leak.

Swordfish

26 May 1941 – the British closed in. The aircraft carrier, HMS *Ark Royal*, launched fifteen bombers, known as *Swordfish* planes, to attack the *Bismarck*, swooping in low, firing torpedoes. To their annoyance every torpedo missed and, equally, to their surprise the *Bismarck* failed to fire back. They soon learnt why – it was not the *Bismarck* they were attacking, but one of their own fleet, the HMS *Sheffield*. Fortunately for the commanders responsible, there were no casualties.

A second batch of *Swordfish* was dispatched and this time they located the *Bismarck* – 600 miles from its intended destination, Saint-Nazaire in northern France. Again the planes flew in low – and twice hit their target. The damage was significant – a torpedo had jammed the ship's rudder. The ship was no longer steering and could do nothing but move around in giant circles.

The Germans dispatched a number of U-boats to assist the flailing ship but Lutjens knew they were too far away to be of any use. The ship was doomed.

All of Germany is with you.

Hitler sent a consolatory message which must have offered little by way of consolation, "All of Germany is with you."

As night fell, the crew upon the stricken ship knew that for most it would be their last night on earth. Captain Lindemann allowed his men a free hand to whatever food and drink they could consume. For others he set the task of building a fake funnel, with the idea that when planted on top of the ship it would alter its silhouette and trick the

British into thinking that the ship was not the *Bismarck* but another vessel. His men must have realised the absurdity of the captain's plan but, nonetheless, thankful for the distraction, threw themselves into the task with gusto.

As dawn broke on 27 May, the battle resumed. The *Bismarck*, battered, impotent and alone, stood little chance. The British fleet pounded her while all the time closing in. At first, the Germans fired back but to no avail. Fires erupted throughout the ship, shells destroyed every lifeboat, and men jumped into the sea to avoid the rising flames as the ship began to capsize.

And still the British closed in. The HMS *Rodney* fired from a distance of less than two miles – in effect shooting from point blank range.

Finally, at ten thirty-nine a.m., the *Bismarck* sank. She may have been scuttled. Men in water swan frantically away, trying to avoid the suction as the ship went under.

Survivors recalled looking back and seeing a heroic and poignant sight – there, on the deck, his hand raised to his white cap, Captain Lindemann saluting as the once mighty ship went down.

Rescue

Two of the British ships were close enough to pick up survivors. But as they went about their noble work, the captain of one of them, the HMS *Dorsetshire*, thought he spied in the distance the tell-tale puff of smoke from a U-boat. Being stationary, his ship presented a sitting target to a U-boat attack and he had no choice but to make a hasty exit. One hundred and ten men had been plucked out of the water, but many, many more were left stranded, screaming for the *Dorsetshire* to come back.

The following morning a German U-boat and a weather ship did appear on the scene but by then all but five of the remaining men had succumbed and died.

1,995 of the *Bismarck*'s crew of 2,200 had lost their lives.

22 June 1941
Hitler Launches Operation Barbarossa, Germany's Invasion of Russia

On 22 June 1941, Adolf Hitler launched Operation Barbarossa, Germany's invasion of the Soviet Union. What followed was a war of annihilation, a horrific clash of totalitarianism, and the most destructive war in history.

Hitler's intention was always to invade the Soviet Union. It was, along with the destruction of the Jews, fundamental to his core objectives – living-space in the east and the subjugation of the Slavic race. He stated his intentions clearly enough in his semi-autobiographical *Mein Kampf*, published in 1925. This was meant to be a war of obliteration – and despite the vastness of Russian territory and manpower, Hitler anticipated a quick victory (his generals had predicted ten weeks). So confident the Nazi hierarchy, that they provided their troops with summer uniforms but made no provision for the fierce Russian winter that lay further ahead.

'You have only to kick in the door,' said Hitler confidently, 'and the whole rotten structure will come crashing down'. Two tons of Iron Crosses were waiting in Germany for those involved with the capture of Moscow. This was always going to be the most brutal war, one which could not be 'conducted with chivalry', as Hitler told his generals, but 'conducted with unprecedented, unmerciful, unrelenting harshness'.

Unprecedented, unmerciful, unrelenting

Two years earlier, on 23 August 1939, the Nazis and Soviets had signed a non-aggression pact. But both sides knew it was never more than a postponement of hostilities. For the Soviets, it gave them time to build up their defences (in the event little was achieved); and for Hitler the pact gave him time to concentrate on the West (the planned defeats of France, Britain and elsewhere) before turning his attention eastwards.

May God Bless Our Weapons

Now, in June 1941, with his Western objectives achieved (with the exception of Britain), the time had come.

On the eve of attack, Joseph Goebbels, Hitler's Minister for Propaganda, wrote in his diary, 'One can hear the breath of history… May God bless our weapons!'

Stalin's spies had forewarned him time and again of the expected attack but he refused to believe it, dismissing it all as 'Hitler's bluff'. When warned of the imminent German invasion from a high-ranking Luftwaffe spy, Stalin responded, 'Tell your "source" to go fuck his mother.' He ordered another shot for spreading 'misinformation'.

German soldier, a fallen Russian and a burning Russian tank, June 1941. German Federal Archives.

Stalin strenuously forbade anything that might appear provocative to the Germans, even insisting on the continuation of Russian food and metal exports to the Germans, as agreed in the 1939 Pact. He prohibited the evacuation of people living near the German border and forbade the setting up of defences.

So when, at four a.m. on 22 June 1941, Operation Barbarossa was launched, progress was rapid. (Barbarossa was the nickname given to Frederick I, 1122-1190, king of Germany and Holy Roman Emperor). At first, more frightened of Stalin's prohibition of 'provocative' acts than the German armies, Soviet soldiers didn't dare fire back. When one desperate Soviet border guard signalled, 'We're being fired on. What do we do?', the response came back, 'You must be mad; and why isn't your signal in code?'

At 6 a.m. that morning, the German Ambassador in Moscow handed over the declaration of war to Vyacheslav Molotov, Stalin's foreign minister. Molotov spat on the piece of paper, tore it up, and ordered his secretary to 'show this gentleman (the ambassador) out through the back door'.

(22 June was not the most auspicious date on which to launch an attack on the Soviet Union. It was on 22 June, exactly one hundred and twenty-nine years before, that Napoleon started his ill-fated invasion of Russia.)

For the good of humanity

Operation Barbarossa was the largest attack ever staged – three and a half million Axis troops, including Romanian and Hungarian, along a 900-mile front from Finland in the north to the Black Sea in the south. The Germans employed their *Blitzkrieg*, or lightning attacks, that had proved so successful against Poland and France. Their tanks were advancing fifty miles a day and, within the first day, one quarter of the Soviet Union's air strength had been destroyed – the Russians had left rows of uncamouflaged planes sat on their airfields, providing easy targets for the *Luftwaffe*.

German soldiers were excited by the prospect of defeating Stalin's mighty Bolshevik empire. One eighteen-year-old German tank driver wrote, 'It's a German's duty for the good of humanity to impose our way of life on lower races and nations'. They, like Hitler, expected an easy victory. An SS sergeant wrote, 'My conviction is that Russia's destruction will take no longer than France's; I assume I'll still get my leave in August'.

By the end of October, Moscow was only sixty-five miles away; over 500,000 square miles of Soviet territory had been captured and, as well as huge numbers of Soviet troops and civilians killed, three million Red Army soldiers had been taken prisoner of war, where, unlike in the West, the rules of captivity held no meaning for the Germans. (Of the five million Soviet PoWs taken during the course of the war, three and a half million were to die of malnutrition, disease and brutality. Those who survived returned home to the Soviet Union to be immediately branded as traitors and, in many instances, sent to the gulags.)

Stalin, once his generals had persuaded him that his country was under attack, controlled the Soviet response. His first acts were to order the execution of those who retreated and to send Molotov to formally announce the war to his people. Molotov's radio broadcast, relayed across cities by loudspeaker, announced this 'act of treachery unprecedented in the history of civilised nations'.

The Great Patriotic War

Stalin attempted to control every aspect of operations but only for the first week before suddenly giving up. 'Lenin founded our state,' he declared, exhausted, 'and we've fucked it up.' This 'bag of bones in a grey tunic', as Nikita Khrushchev later described him, disappeared to his dacha where, many believe, he suffered a mental breakdown. Nothing could be done without him, nothing issued in the way of direction.

When, after three days, his Politburo came for him, Stalin feared he was about to be arrested. Instead, they came to ask him what to do. Once stirred, Stalin re-emerged. On 3 July, in his first public address since the invasion, perhaps the most important speech of his life, Stalin spoke of 'The Great Patriotic War'.

By the end of June, Finland, Hungary and Albania had all declared war on the USSR. For Finland it was a 'holy war', an opportunity to avenge their defeat the previous year during the Finnish-Soviet 'Winter War'.

Joseph Stalin, August 1945. US Army Signal Corps.

The sides had been drawn, the invasion launched. What followed was the most ferocious war ever known which was to last three years and claim the lives of over five million Axis troops, nine million Soviet troops, and up to twenty million civilian deaths.

7 November 1941
The Sinking of a Hospital ship

On the 7 November 1941, the Soviet hospital ship, the *Armenia*, was torpedoed and sunk by the Germans. It was one of the worst maritime disasters in history. All but eight of the 7,000 passengers perished on a ship designed for not more than a thousand. A comparatively modest 1,514 died on the *Titanic* (1912) and 1,198 on the *Lusitania* (1915) yet the sinking of the *Armenia* is all but lost to history.

Sunk in the Black Sea, the exact location of the wreck is still a mystery and for years, the question remained – was a hospital ship, identified by a Red Cross, a legitimate target?

A stricken city

Designed for 980 passengers and crew, over seven times that number had surged onto the ship in the Crimean port of Yalta that fateful night of 7 November 1941. The reason was blind panic. The Nazi war machine, which had invaded the Soviet Union less than five months before, had overrun the Crimean peninsula and was bearing down on Yalta. People expected the city to fall within a matter of hours. The only possible means of escape for its stricken population was by sea – the roads outside the city having been sealed off by the Germans.

Built in Leningrad in 1928, the double-decker *Armenia* began its career as a passenger ship. In August 1941, following the outbreak of war, it was pressed into military service as a hospital ship. The day before its sinking, the *Armenia* had left the port of Sevastopol having taken civilian evacuees and the occupants of several military hospitals. Crammed with up to 5,000 passengers, the ship made for Tuapse, a town on the northeast coast of the Black Sea, about two hundred and fifty miles east. But the captain, Captain Vladimir Plaushevsky, received orders to pick up extra people from nearby Yalta.

More civilians and wounded soldiers, some severely, crammed onto the ship amid scenes of chaos and utter panic. No register was taken, no names recorded of these additional two thousand passengers. Captain Plaushevsky then received orders to remain in port until escort vessels were at hand to chaperon him out. The delay frustrated the captain, he had to get going, they were cutting it too fine.

Torpedoed

The next morning, seven o'clock, the *Armenia* finally set sail, escorted by two armed boats and two fighter planes.

The escorts were unable to prevent a German torpedo bomber, a Heinkel He-111, swooping-in low and firing two torpedoes at the ship. It was eleven twenty-nine a.m., the ship was twenty-five miles into its journey. The first torpedo missed but the second one scored a splitting the ship into two. The *Armenia* sunk w.. four minutes. All but eight of the 7,000 passengers die the survivors being picked up by a patrol boat.

The tragedy lay in the postponement of its departure. If Captain Plaushevsky had not lost those precious hours, the ship may well have arrived at its intended destination.

Lying at a depth of about 480 metres, the location of the *Armenia* wreck remains unknown despite the efforts of oceanic explorer, Robert Ballard, discoverer of several historical wrecks including the aforementioned *Titanic* and *Lusitania*.

A legitimate target?

Was the *Armenia* a legitimate target? As a hospital ship, it was clearly marked with the Red Cross, both on its sides and, clearly visible to the German pilots, on the deck. But it had a military escort, and it had two of its own anti-aircraft guns, so under the rules of war, it was a perfectly acceptable target.

But this doesn't detract from the catastrophe of its sinking and today we should remember, if only momentarily, the forgotten tragedy of the *Armenia*.

29 November 1941
The Execution of **Zoya Kosmodemyanskaya**

On 29 November 1941, Zoya Kosmodemyanskaya, aged eighteen, was executed by the Nazis.

The Nazis had invaded the Soviet Union on 22 June 1941 and by late November had surrounded and laid siege to Leningrad and were bearing down on Moscow. The Soviet authorities were recruiting volunteers to break through the German lines and operate as partisan fighters in German-occupied areas. Their task, generally, was to cause as much disruption to the German advance. It was a dangerous assignment but one which eighteen-year-old Zoya readily volunteered for.

Zoya Kosmodemyanskaya was born 13 September 1923 in the district of Tambov, about three hundred miles southeast of Moscow. She was well-cultured and devoured the works of Tolstoy, Dickens, Shakespeare, Goethe and Pushkin and loved the music of Tchaikovsky and Beethoven, and was a member of the Soviet youth komsomol organisation. (Pictured below is Zoya's komsomol membership card).

Partisan

Having been accepted as a partisan, despite her tender age, Zoya was given the name 'Tanya'. Handed a revolver and trained how to use it, she was assigned to a small group of partisans and given instructions. Their first task was to lay mines on the Volokolamsk highway, just behind German lines, about 80 miles west of Moscow. Excited and nervous, Zoya declared, 'If we fall, let's fall like heroes'.

Another task involved laying spikes in the road but the more dangerous jobs were reserved for the young men. Zoya pleaded her case, stating, 'Difficulties ought to be shared equally.' Her commander, a man who went by the name of Boris, acquiesced.

Thus, on 27 November, Zoya was sent into Petrischevo, a village occupied and brimming with Germans. She went alone while Boris and his team waited anxiously for her return. After a few hours, Zoya emerged from the woods, triumphant at having burnt down a house and a stable. However, unbeknownst to Zoya, a village collaborator had spotted her and told the Germans.

The following day, Zoya returned to the village. This time, she didn't return. After three days, Boris knew that she was dead.

What happened to Zoya is based on a report written by a Soviet journalist, Pyotr Lidov, pieced together from various eyewitness statements and published in the Soviet newspaper, *Pravda* ('Truth'), on 27 January 1942. Lidov returned to Petrischevo shortly after its recapture by the Soviets and spoke to various villagers about what had happened during the brief spell of German occupation.

'You can't hang us all'

The story that emerged was how, courtesy of the information provided by the collaborator, a young girl was caught red-handed setting light to a stable. The Germans dragged her off and interrogated her at length while beating her with their belts, punching her, burning her with lighters, and cutting the skin on her back with a handsaw. One overheard exchange went as follows:

'Who are you?' 'I won't tell you.' 'Was it you who set fire to the stables?' 'Yes it was.' 'Why did you do it?' 'To destroy you.'

A German sergeant, later taken prison-of-war, described the scene:

'The young Russian heroine remained tight-lipped. She would not betray her friends. She turned blue with the cold, blood flowed from her wounds, but still she said nothing... Her lips were bloody and swollen. She'd evidently bitten them when her captors had tried to wring a confession from her.'

During the night, they forced her outside, barefoot, in sub-zero temperatures.

Zoya was hung on the morning of 29 November 1941. The Germans placed a sign round her neck, saying, 'Incendiary'. The Germans gathered around, some with cameras at the ready, and ordered the villagers to witness the scene. Perched on a box, with the rope around her neck, she called out to the villagers, 'Comrades! Why are you so gloomy? I am not afraid to die! I am happy to die for my people!' Then, as a final act of defiance, she cried, 'You'll hang me now, but I am not alone. There are two hundred million of us. You can't hang us all.' The box was then kicked away from beneath her.

The Germans took photographs of Zoya's body, her breasts mutilated, as she lay dead on the ground. When the photos were later taken off captured Germans and published with Lidov's article, it caused a national sensation within the Soviet Union.

Her body was left to hang for many weeks, the villagers forbidden to remove it. A new unit of Germans, passing through on New Year's Eve, subjected Zoya's corpse to more indignities. Finally, in New Year 1942, she was buried.

'The people's heroine'

On reading Lidov's article in *Pravda*, Stalin reputably remarked. 'Here is the people's heroine'. She was bestowed the award, 'Hero of the Soviet Union' and immediately eulogised throughout the country. Poems, plays, novels and films were made of her life, streets and buildings named after her. To this day, the name Zoya Kosmodemyanskaya is known throughout Russia.

In the 1990s, following the collapse of the Soviet Union, the myth of the teenage heroine began to be questioned – were there ever German troops stationed in Petrischevo; was Zoya killed by Germans or by Soviets resentful at her burning their buildings and dwellings? Was it even Zoya's body or that of another missing partisan?

More recently, the doubters have been silenced and the memory and legacy of Zoya Kosmodemyanskaya **endures** to this day.

7 December 1941,
Pearl Harbor, the Day of Infamy

How Japan's hollow victory spelt the end for Hitler

On 7 December 1941, Japan launched a surprise attack on the US. In just two hours it destroyed a large part of the US fleet docked in Pearl Harbor and, in one stroke, forever destroyed US isolationism and made the conflict global.

The US may have been expecting war but the attack on Pearl Harbor still took it totally by surprise. Yet eleven months before, a lone voice had predicted such a possibility. On the 27 January 1941, the US ambassador in Japan, Joseph Grew, cabled the White House warning that the Japanese *might* 'attempt a surprise attack on Pearl Harbor using all their military facilities'.

As 1941 wore on, the likelihood of war became more apparent but the US ignored Grew's prediction, believing that conflict, if it came, would either start in the US-controlled Philippines or the Dutch or British possessions in Southeast Asia.

Certainly, US president, Franklin D. Roosevelt, believed war was a distinct possibility – 'They [the Japanese] hate us,' he said privately. 'Sooner or later, they're going to come after us'. He also feared what would happen to the US if Japan overran Britain's possessions in the Southeast Asia – 'If Great Britain goes down,' Roosevelt said, 'all of us in all the Americas would be living at the point of a gun.'

The USS Arizona *under attack, Pearl Harbor, 7 December 1941. National Archives and Records Administration.*

Asia for the Asians

On 17 October 1941 the prospect of war became more real – Japan's prime minister, Fumimaro Konoye, known for his restraint and sense of compromise, was replaced by the more aggressive Hideki Tojo. Within a month, Tojo had finalized plans to cripple the US fleet, and invade much of Southeast Asia to secure for Japan its supply of natural resources. Japan had long wanted to rid the area of Western imperialists and rule Asia on behalf of its neighbours – 'Asia for the Asians' became its war cry.

On 26 November, Tojo's plan went into action – a Japanese fleet commanded by Admiral Isoruku Yamamoto, consisting of six aircraft carriers, two battleships and assorted other craft, set off from north-eastern Japan. The Americans had broken Japanese codes but in the event this gave them no advantage as the US fleet was maintaining strict radio silence. Meanwhile, in Washington, the US and Japan were negotiating Japan's withdrawal from China. (Japan and China had been at war since 1931). Japan had no intention of withdrawing but was happy to lure the US into thinking that their intentions were honourable. It was all part of the ruse.

With Yamamoto's fleet 275 miles north of the Hawaiian island of Oahu, the first wave of fighters took off, commanded by Lt Commander Mitsuo Fuchida (twenty-five years later, having converted to Christianity, Fuchida became a US citizen). It took them one and a half hours to reach Oahu. At one point dense cloud obscured their route but at the most opportune moment, the clouds parted, and there below them was Pearl Harbor.

Tora, tora, tora!

It was approaching 7 a.m. on Sunday 7 December when the radar station on Oahu first reported to its HQ a number of aircraft on its screen. The reply came back: 'Don't worry about it'. HQ was expecting a squadron of US planes from California to be arriving that same morning. But these were Japanese planes (bombers, dive-bombers and fighters), 181 of them, intent on ripping out the heart of the US fleet quietly moored on this Pacific island, 3,400 miles away from Japan.

Neatly and conveniently lined up along 'Battleship Row', were seven of the US's eight battleships plus a hundred other ships. Fuchida, knowing he couldn't fail, dispatched the pre-arranged victory signal, *Tora, tora, tora* (Tiger, tiger, tiger). Torpedoes and bombs rained down. The general alarm sounded, 'Man your battle stations – THIS IS NO DRILL!' Within minutes, several of the ships had been hit. Men jumped overboard and tried to swim to safety. The previously calm waters of the harbour, now glazed with a layer of oil, erupted into a wall of flame, killing many of those in the water.

The biggest casualty, claiming 1,177 lives, almost half of the victims at Pearl Harbor, was the battleship, the USS *Arizona*. Twenty-three sets of brothers died aboard the ship, plus all twenty-one members of the *Arizona*'s music band. Hit four times by Japanese bombers, the ship's magazine exploded with such intensity that it lifted the entire battleship ten feet out of the water and knocked down people two miles away.

The nearby airfields were also targeted. Row upon row of perfectly-lined aircraft were destroyed. American sailors, queuing up for breakfast and unable to comprehend what was happening, were mowed down as they waited their turn.

At 8.40, the second wave attacked. The Americans, now employing their anti-aircraft guns, managed to hit a few of the incoming planes, but the Japanese fighters inflicted yet more damage.

By 10 a.m. it was all over – three of the eight American battleships had been sunk and four seriously damaged; many other vessels were destroyed together with almost three hundred planes. 2,403 Americans died (civilian and military) and over 1,000 wounded. The Japanese lost twenty-nine planes and a hundred pilots.

One American admiral admitted to the Americans' preconceived racial stereotyping: 'At first I thought the U.S. Army Air Corps was accidentally bombing us. We were so proud, so vain, and so ignorant of Japanese capability. It never entered our consciousness that they'd have the temerity to attack us. We knew the Japanese didn't see well, especially at night – we knew this as a matter of fact. We knew they couldn't build good weapons, they made junky equipment, they just imitated us. All we had to do was get out there and sink them. It turns out they could see better than we could and their torpedoes, unlike ours, worked'.

At the same time, Japanese forces had attacked the Philippines and the British colony of Hong Kong and violated neutral Thailand. The Pacific islands of Wake and Midway also fell victim to attack as well as British-controlled Malaya. Singapore, on the southern tip of Malaya, had been bombed. Without an official declaration of war, Japan, in just a matter of hours, had secured control of the skies and seas of a quarter of the world's surface. As Winston Churchill described in his war memoirs, 'Over all this vast expanse of waters Japan was supreme, and we everywhere were weak and naked.'

The Sleeping Enemy

But as successful as the operation may have appeared, its triumph was short-lived – a third wave, due to attack the huge stores of fuel and its navy arsenal, was cancelled due to fear of an American counterattack, and the battleships, having been sunk only in the shallow waters of the harbour, were mostly repaired and fully operational before the end of the war (although the USS *Arizona*, for one, remained on the bottom of the harbour where it is still today). None of the aircraft carriers had been hit nor the submarines. While Japan celebrated its supposed victory, Yamamoto knew that in the long term he had failed – 'a military man can scarcely pride himself on having smitten a sleeping enemy'.

The following day, in his address to Congress, Roosevelt declared, 'Yesterday, December 7, 1941, a date which will live in infamy, the United States of America was suddenly and deliberately attacked by naval and air forces of the Empire of Japan'. Congress accordingly voted 470 to 1 to go to war (the one being a pacifist vote from Montana).

Churchill was delighted. 'To have the United States at our side' (he later wrote), 'was to me the greatest joy. Now at this very moment I knew the United States was in the war, up to the neck and in to the death. So we had won after all!... Hitler's fate was sealed. Mussolini's fate was sealed. As for the Japanese, they would be ground to powder.'

Hitler Declares War

Adolf Hitler too was pleased, the teetotaller breaking with habit and toasting the Honorary Aryans, as he called the Japanese, with a small glass of champagne. 'Now it is impossible for us to lose the war,' he announced with glee. On 11 December, less than six months since invading the Soviet Union, Germany declared war on the US. Hitler had not been obliged to – the Tripartite Pact, signed by Germany, Italy and Japan in September 1940, had only stipulated that Germany would declare war if Japan was the *victim* of aggression.

But Hitler wanted to pre-empt the possibility of the US declaring war on Germany. After all, as his Foreign Minister, Joachim von Ribbentrop, explained, 'A great power does not allow itself to be declared war upon; it declares war on others'. Hitler, always hostile to America with its racially diverse and therefore inferior population, believed Germany had nothing to fear, predicting that the US would not be ready for war until at least 1970.

Both acts, the invasion of the Soviet Union and the declaration of war against the US, stand up as Hitler's two greatest blunders. Germany's fate was sealed and the conflict, that had started twenty-seven months before, was now truly global.

20 January 1942
The Wannsee Conference

On 20 January 1942 took place one of the most notorious meeting in history. In a grand villa on the picturesque banks of Berlin's Lake Wannsee, met fifteen high-ranking Nazis. Chaired by the chief of the security police, thirty-seven-year-old Reinhard Heydrich, the fifteen men represented various agencies of the Nazi apparatus.

'Final Solution of the Jewish Question'

Reinhard Heydrich's objective, as tasked by Hermann Göring (and therefore, presumably, Adolf Hitler), was to secure the support of these various agencies for the implementation of the 'Final Solution of the Jewish Question', the systematic annihilation of the European Jew.

Goring's letter to Heydrich, dated July 1941, states, *'I hereby command you to make all necessary organizational, functional, and material preparations for a complete solution of the Jewish Question in the German sphere of influence in Europe.'*).

The mass murder of Jews was already taking place. The initial method of shooting Jews on the edges of pits was considered too time-consuming and detrimental on the mental health of the murder squads. The squads, often recruited from the local populations in conquered areas, willingly collaborated in the killings but eventually found the task gruelling. Seeking alternative methods, the Germans began experimenting with gas, using carbon monoxide in mobile units, but although better this was still considered too slow and inefficient. Eventually, after experiments on Soviet prisoners of war in Auschwitz during September 1941, Zyklon B gas was discovered as a rapid and efficient means of murder.

The Wannsee Conference, as it became known, discussed escalating the killing to a new, industrial level. Heydrich estimated that eleven million Jews still resided in Europe and needed to be "combed from West to East." He produced a list of nations and their respective number of Jews, not only in countries already under Nazi occupation but also neutral nations and those not yet occupied. For example, Britain, according to Heydrich's figures, contained 330,000 Jews; Sweden 8,000; Spain 6,000; Switzerland 18,000; and Ireland 4,000, plus two hundred Jews in Albania.

Eliminated through natural reduction

The more able-bodied Jews, said Heydrich, would be used for labour "whereby a large number will doubtlessly be eliminated through natural reduction." Those that survived the labour, the toughest, would, if liberated, be the "core of a new Jewish revival," therefore they had to be "dealt with appropriately." The minutes of the meeting, written up by Adolf Eichmann, were littered with such euphemisms but, according to Eichmann at his trial in 1962, once the official meeting had finished, they spoke openly of executions and liquidation.

No one at the meeting objected or questioned the proposals, and Heydrich hadn't expected any but nonetheless was pleased with the level of enthusiasm. The rest of the meeting discussed definitions of 'Jewishness' – to what extent persons of mixed blood could be defined as Jewish; and whether children born of mixed marriages (German and Jew) were Jewish or not. And veterans of the First World War, it was decided, would be sent to ghettos specifically for the aged.

Satisfied, Heydrich drew the meeting to a close. The men retired to comfortable chairs to smoke, drink brandy and gossip whilst admiring the view over the lake. The meeting, barely an hour and a half long, was over.

Postscript

Hitler had admired Reinhard Heydrich, the 'man with the iron heart' as he called him and, in September 1941, appointed him in charge of Nazi-occupied Czechoslovakia. Heydrich's ruthlessness in dealing with the Jews within his 'protectorate' won him the sobriquet 'the Butcher of Prague'. On 27 May 1942, only four months after the Wannsee Conference, Heydrich was the victim of an ambush set up by four Czech resistance fighters. A week later he died of his injuries and was given a state funeral in Berlin. The reprisals in Czechoslovakia were, predictably, savage.

Following the war, Adolf Eichmann escaped to Argentina where he was eventually hunted down. His trial provided fresh details on the workings within the Nazi hierarchy. He was executed in on 31 May 1962.

15 February 1942
The Fall of Singapore

With the fall of Singapore on 15 February 1942, Britain suffered the worst humiliation in its military history.

The photograph sums it up: General Arthur Percival (far right), the British commander in Malaya, and his fellow officers, walking forlornly towards the Japanese commanders to sign the dismal surrender. With their baggy shorts, knee-length socks and tin helmets, one carries the Union Jack while another holds the white flag of surrender. Escorting them, a number of Japanese soldiers, or 'little men' as the British military elite referred to them.

The 'Gibraltar of the East'

British Malaya had been considered a strategic stronghold within the eastern Empire, and the island of Singapore, 273 square miles, on the southern tip of Malaya, was known as the 'Gibraltar of the East'. Acquired by Stamford Raffles for Britain's East India Company in 1819, Singapore became a full British possession five years later, in 1824. Colonial life in early twentieth century Singapore was one of tea, tennis and dancing. Rumours of a Japanese attack were dismissed as nonsense; these 'Japs' with their feeble eyes could hardly shoot straight, let alone pose a threat to the might of the Malayan-based British troops and their Commonwealth comrades.

An impressive naval defence system consisting of huge guns had been built at great cost during the 1920s facing south out to sea. To the north of the island, on the mainland, lay hundreds of miles of dense Malayan jungle and rubber plantations considered by the British to be impenetrable. Stationed on the island, almost 100,000 British, Canadian, Australian, Indian and a few local Malay troops.

'I never received a more direct shock'

The situation seemed even more secure when, on 2 December 1941, two British warships, the HMS's *Prince of Wales* and *Repulse*, escorted by four destroyers, made their presence felt in Singapore's harbour. No one seemed too perturbed that the ships lacked air support – the aircraft carrier carrying almost fifty Hurricanes had run aground and needed three weeks of repair.

But things were far from secure. First, on 7 December, at the same time as their comrades were launching their attack on Pearl Harbor, the Japanese landed on Malaya on the north-eastern coast near the city of Kota Bahru. By the following day they had secured their first foothold on the Malayan peninsula.

Two days later, on 10 December, eighty-eight Japanese planes attacked the *Prince of Wales* and *Repulse* and their escorting destroyers. Without the benefit of air support, the British ships were easily torpedoed and sunk with the loss of 840 lives. 1,285 survivors were taken prisoner. The Japanese, in turn, lost only four planes. Years later, Winston Churchill wrote, 'In all the war, I never received a more direct shock.'

Bad for morale

On Malaya itself, the Japanese advanced south from Kota Bahru with their infantry soldiers on bicycles, and using tanks which the British had thought totally impractical within the dense jungle, and all ably supported by fighter planes. Their aim: to conquer Malaya and capture the island of Singapore on the southern tip of the mainland, 620 miles to the south.

However, the British were not, at this stage, overly concerned, overestimating the defensive nature of the jungle and underestimating the character of the Japanese soldier. Until early January 1942, Arthur Percival (pictured below) prohibited the building of defences on Singapore's north coast, believing that to do so would be bad for morale.

But within six weeks of landing in Malaya, the Japanese, with total air superiority, were within striking distance of Singapore. Unaware of how numerically inferior the enemy, an impressive bluff perpetuated by the Japanese commander, General Tomoyuki Yamashita, the British and Commonwealth troops panicked at the speed of the Japanese advance. On 31 January, Percival ordered his troops off Malaya to Singapore. Retreating, his troops partially destroyed the causeway over the mile-wide Johore Strait between the mainland and the island.

A contingent of Australian troops, too wounded to move, was left lying within the Malayan jungle, calmly smoking. The Japanese, having rounded them up, decapitated them.

With the loss of only 2,000 of his men, Yamashita (pictured) had conquered Malaya in little more than seven weeks. Now there was just the small matter of Singapore. But Yamashita was worried – his supply lines were stretched, he was lacking ammunition and with only 20,000 men, his forces were outnumbered.

But it was the British resolve that collapsed. Panic set in as the Japanese bombed the island and

Singapore city was flattened. Civilians tried all means to escape, fighting one another for the remaining places on the last ships and planes heading out, including accounts of desperate men securing their places by gunpoint.

Meanwhile, on 8 February, the Japanese had repaired the causeway. The way ahead was clear. Two days later, Yamashita sent Percival a letter demanding their surrender.

'Defeated by an army of clever gangsters'

On 10 February, Churchill ordered: 'The battle must be fought to the bitter end at all costs… Commanders and senior officers should die with their troops. The honour of the British Empire and the British Army is at stake.'

Percival reiterated the Prime Minster's order the following day: 'In some units the troops have not shown the fighting spirit expected of men of the British Empire. … It will be a lasting disgrace if we are defeated by an army of clever gangsters many times inferior in numbers to our men.'

The British, although running short of food and water, were well equipped with ammunition, unlike the Japanese who were fast running out. And with 80,000 men at his disposal, Percival's cause, on paper, seemed favourable. But despite Churchill's unusually severe missive, British discipline broke, panic set in, and the cause was lost. Those under him urged Percival to surrender to save further loss of life. The last ships had gone – there was no escape as the Japanese rampaged, showing no mercy to either soldier or civilian, bayoneting and killing women, children, hospital patients and all they came across. The worst atrocity occurred at the Alexandra military hospital, where the Japanese first bayoneted to death a British officer carrying a white flag, then proceeded to massacre 320 staff, nurses and patients, including soldiers undergoing surgery.

Capitulation

By 12 February, eighty percent of the island lay in Japanese hands. Percival was not to know that the Japanese were down to the last few hour's worth of ammunition. Finally, with the situation lost and the prospect of a counterattack impossible, Percival surrendered. It was the 15 February 1942, and the fall of Singapore was, in Churchill's words, the 'worst disaster and largest capitulation in British history'. (Pictured above: victorious Japanese troops marching through Singapore's city centre).

The myth of the invincibility of the European soldier was shattered and over 80,000 British and Commonwealth troops were to spend the rest of the war in captivity. Half of them would never return home.

The island endured three and half years of brutal Japanese occupation which included a massacre of its Chinese population, a massacre that was to claim up to 50,000 lives. The island was to remain under occupation until soon after Japan's surrender in August 1945.

28 March 1942
The Raid on Saint-Nazaire

'It was one of those enterprises which could be attempted only because in the eyes of the enemy it was absolutely impossible,' said Lord Louis Mountbatten, Chief of Combined Operations, describing the Second World War raid on Saint-Nazaire.

On 28 March 1942, 621 men of the Royal navy and British Commandos attacked the port of Saint-Nazaire in occupied France. The mission has been dubbed 'the greatest raid of all time.' It was certainly daring, audacious in the extreme and terribly dangerous – less than half the men returned alive. Five Victoria Crosses were awarded, two of them posthumously.

A Bleak Time

Early 1942 was a bleak time for the Western Allies during the Second World War – British forces had just surrendered their garrison at Singapore; Britain was losing the Battle of the Atlantic; and wartime austerity was beginning to bite. In Europe, following the fall of France eighteen months earlier, Nazi occupation had been firmly established; and the first deportations of Jews residing in France had just begun.

Britain's high command was gripped by fear of Germany's huge battleship, the *Tirpitz*, a massive ship, a sixth of a mile long. Its sister ship, the *Bismarck*, had been sunk in May 1941, but the *Tirpitz* still roamed large. The only dry dock on the French coast capable of accommodating such a ship was to be found at the port Saint-Nazaire, a town of some 50,000 people. If the Normandie dock, as it was called, the largest dry dock in the world at the time, could be put out of action, then the *Tirpitz*'s activity in the Atlantic would be severely constrained.

The Plan

Thus, in late February 1942, the British command settled on their objective – to attack Saint-Nazaire. They had only four weeks to devise and execute the plan before the spring tides turned against them. The problem, however, was that the port was heavily defended by the occupying Germans. The idea of an aerial bombardment was immediately rejected because of potential French civilian casualties. The plan they came up with instead was to ram an 'expendable vessel' packed with timed explosives into the Normandie dock and destroy it. The vessel they found was old American destroyer, the HMS *Campbeltown*, built in 1919 and now obsolete. And so Operation Chariot came into being. The force involved two additional escort destroyers and sixteen smaller ships.

Pictured: two of the participating commandos: Corporal Bert Shipton, left, and Sergeant 'Dai' Davis.

Commandos on board the *Campbeltown* would jump off the ship, attack dock installations, pumping stations and the U-boat pens, plus a nearby power station, bridges, and locks, before meeting up at a spot called Old Mole to re-embark on a number of Motor Launches and head home. Sending a small force against a heavily-defended dock needed the element of surprise.

The attack would involve 621 men, a mixture of Royal Navy and commandos. They were to be split into three teams – assault, demotion and protection. The wartime commandos had been established in 1940, conceived in the 'midst of failure' following the loss of the British Expeditionary Force at Dunkirk. Their task was to carry out small but daring raids against the territories of Nazi-occupied Europe. But this, the raid on Saint-Nazaire, would be the most daring yet.

In preparation for her final journey, HMS *Campbeltown* was modified to make her lighter and, by removing two of her four funnels, to make her look more like a German destroyer.

28 March 1942

And so at two p.m. on 26 March, the convoy set off from Falmouth in Cornwall. All but the most senior knew nothing about the mission until they had boarded and were on their way to France. Many suffered from seasickness; others prayed. Two Scots changed out of their trousers and into kilts – if they were to die, they said, they wanted to be properly dressed. Despite knowing they were embarking on a suicidal mission, the overall atmosphere was 'calm, confident and cheerful'.

Just minutes from their target, the *Campbeltown* was spotted by German searchlights. Warning shots were fired but the ship was able to return a message using German codes, winning them a couple of invaluable minutes before the Germans realized they had been duped. A firefight ensued. Thus, under heavy and sustained fire, the destroyer, packed with 4.5 tons of explosives, picked up speed and still managed to ram the gates of the Normandie dock.

Although the raid came as a complete shock to the Germans, they reacted quickly, pouring troops into the port. Gunfights took place all around the docks and in the streets of the town. As the convoy prepared to retreat, having completed its objectives, a number of men were still unaccounted for. Many had been killed, others were forced into surrendering; five of them managed to slip into the French countryside and eventually made their way all the way down to neutral Spain, and from there, back to England. Most of the smaller ships had been destroyed.

(Pictured, the HMS Campbeltown *rammed against the dock gates shortly before exploding).*

Meanwhile, German officers inspected HMS *Campbeltown* smashed up against the dock gates. At noon, on 28 March, the timed explosives detonated causing a huge explosion and further destroying the dock. 360 Germans were killed. The dock remained out of commission for the rest of the war and indeed was not fully operational again for over a decade.

Aftermath

The raid had been a complete success in that all its objectives had been realized. But the cost was heavy: of the 621 commandos and sailors who participated in the raid, only 228 made it back to England; 169 were killed and a further two hundred and fifteen were taken prisoner.

There were awards aplenty to acknowledge the sacrifice and astonishing bravery – eighty-nine medals were awarded, including five Victoria Crosses (two posthumously).

The raid gave Britons hope at a low point in their history. It was a 'gutsy plan, requiring luck, bluff and surprise in abundance to come off'; a plan that had a 'chance of succeeding by virtue of its very audacity'. The raid certainly left the Germans feeling vulnerable – after all, the enemy had managed to penetrate even their stoutest of defences. Seven months later, on 18 October 1942, Hitler issued his infamous 'Commando Order'. In direct violation of the rules of war, it commanded the immediate execution of any captured commando, even those wearing uniform and attempting to surrender.

And what of the much-feared *Tirpitz*? As hoped, she never again ventured into Atlantic waters, confining herself to the Norwegian fjords where she was sunk by the RAF on 12 November 1944.

15 April 1942
Malta Receives a Medal

On 15 April 1942, Malta received Britain's highest civilian award for gallantry, the George Cross. But why would an island receive a medal?

Lying halfway between Italy and North Africa, the 120 square-mile island of Malta unwittingly played a pivotal role during the North African campaign in World War Two.

Part of the British Empire since 1814, the island was Britain's only military base in the central Mediterranean.

Italian bombing

On 10 June 1940, Italy entered the war and on the following day began by bombing Malta. The British garrison on the island defended the population, and supplies and extra planes were shipped in. But it was only the start.

British submarines and Hurricane fighter planes retaliated by attacking Italian and German convoys, which were shipping men and equipment to North Africa. In October 1941 Erwin Rommel, the German commander in North Africa, lost over sixty percent of his supplies to British forces based in Malta.

Now the Germans

The Germans decided that Malta was causing too much damage and Albert Kesselring, Hitler's Mediterranean commander, promised to "wipe Malta off the map." Luftwaffe and U-boats stationed sixty miles north on the island of Sicily launched aerial attacks on Malta and the siege intensified. Supplies to the island virtually ceased and the inhabitants suffered eighteen months of hunger as well as continual bombardment. Civilians, starved and frightened, packed the caves beneath the capital Valletta.

It was during this time of deprivation that Britain's King George VI awarded the island, as a collective, the George Cross "to bear witness to the heroism and devotion that will long be famous in history".

In May 1942 the British tried to fly in a contingent of Spitfires but most were destroyed before they could be deployed. With food and supplies nearly exhausted, the future looked bleak. Ammunition was so low that only a few rounds were allowed to be fired per day.

Spitfire to the rescue

A second attempt to bring in Spitfires was successful. Immediately they went on the offensive against the German Luftwaffe and were able to escort supply convoys through to the besieged islanders. A convoy of merchant ships escorted by Spitfires and warships managed to survive intense German attack and arrived in Valletta on 15 August, the Maltese feast day of St Mary. Their survival and arrival on this important day of the Maltese calendar were seen as nothing less than heaven-sent. The worst was over.

Renewed attacks from Malta on Rommel's supplies severely hampered the German campaign in Egypt, and by the end of 1942, British supplies to the island were arriving unmolested. The siege was over and the island had survived.

The Maltese flag

The George Cross to Malta was the first time it had been awarded to a collective. (The second and, so far, last occasion was in 1999 when it was awarded to the Royal Ulster Constabulary.) To this day the image of the George Cross appears in the top left corner of the Maltese flag.

Bernard Montgomery

The son of a bishop, Bernard Montgomery, or 'Monty', was born in London but spent his early years in Tasmania. He fought during much of the First World War, and was twice badly wounded. An obstinate individual, he fell out with his mother to such an extent that when she died in 1949, he refused to attend her funeral. Training to be an army officer at Sandhurst he was demoted for having set a fellow student on fire and during First World War he allegedly caught a German by kneeing him in the testicles.

The early death of his wife in 1937 from septicemia, caused by an insect bite, devastated Monty and from then on, he devoted himself entirely to his career.

El Alamein

Self-confident in the extreme, prone to odd headwear, Montgomery was adored by his men, especially during the Second World War desert campaigns in North Africa during which he made his name by defeating Erwin

Rommel at El Alamein. But he frequently clashed with his American counterparts and, because of his immense self-pride, took offence easily. Having planned the successful invasion of Sicily, he believed himself worthy of being in overall command of the Italian campaign, and took great umbrage at having to work under Dwight Eisenhower.

In December 1943, Montgomery was appointed land commander, again under Eisenhower, for Operation Overlord, the planned invasion of France. His D-Day objectives included the capture of Caen within the first 24 hours. In the event, it took several weeks and proved costly, for which he was heavily criticised. During the chaotic days of mid-June, his American counterparts felt that Montgomery's strategy was too cautious and hoped to have him replaced, a view endorsed by Churchill.

But Montgomery held onto his post and his tactics did draw much enemy attention to the east of the Allies' bridgehead, allowing the Americans to successfully breakout from the west.

Towards Berlin

He clashed with Eisenhower again over how to proceed through Germany. Montgomery energetically advocated a narrow push, a 'pencil-thrust', but Eisenhower's preference for a broad thrust prevailed. Montgomery's carefully planned airborne assault on Arnhem in 1944 ended disastrously, and again costly, but his efforts in relieving the beleaguered Americans during the Battle of the Bulge helped restore his reputation.

Montgomery resented Eisenhower being given the responsibility of land operations for the push into Germany. He believed Eisenhower's 'ignorance as to how to run a war is absolute and complete'. On 4 May 1945, at Lüneburg Heath in Lower Saxony, Montgomery formally accepted the surrender of all German forces in north-western Europe.

Post-war

Post-war, Montgomery worked as Chief of the Imperial General Staff until, in 1951, he joined the newly-formed NATO, becoming Deputy Supreme Commander, a post he retained until his retirement seven years later.

When, during his retirement, he was asked to name the three greatest generals in history, he replied, 'The other two were Alexander the Great and Napoleon'. He wrote his memoirs in which he criticized many of his former colleagues and commanders.

Bernard Montgomery died on 24 March 1976, aged eighty-eight.

19 August 1942
The Dieppe Raid

In August 1942, Winston Churchill, Great Britain's wartime prime minister, flew to Moscow and there met for the first time the Soviet leader, Joseph Stalin. Fourteen months before, on 22 June 1941, Hitler had launched Operation Barbarossa, Germany's invasion of the Soviet Union, the largest military invasion ever conducted. Almost immediately, Stalin was urging Churchill to open a second front by attacking Nazi-occupied Europe from the West, thereby forcing Hitler to divert troops to the west and alleviating in part the enormous pressure the Soviet Union found itself under. Now, as Churchill prepared to meet Stalin, German forces were bearing down on the strategically and symbolically important Russian city of Stalingrad.

Churchill knew that if Germany were to defeat the Soviet Union then Hitler would be able to concentrate his whole military strength on the west. But although tentative plans for a large-scale invasion were afoot, to act too quickly, too hastily, would be foolhardy. Churchill withstood Stalin's pressure. There would be no second front for at least another year. But, in the meanwhile, Churchill was able to offer a 'reconnaissance in force' on the French port of Dieppe, with the objective of drawing away German troops from the Eastern Front. Whether Stalin was at all appeased by this morsel of compensation, Churchill does not say.

Operation Jubilee

Pictured: German soldiers defending the French port of Dieppe against the Anglo-Canadian raid, 19 August 1942.

Thus, in the early hours of 19 August 1942, the Allies launched Operation Jubilee – the raid on Dieppe, sixty-five miles across from England. 252 ships crossed the Channel in a five-pronged attack carrying tanks together with 5,000 Canadians and 1,000 British and American troops plus a handful of fighters from the French resistance. Nearing their destination, one prong ran into a German merchant convoy. A skirmish ensued. More fatally, it meant that the element of surprise had been lost – aware of what was taking place, the Germans at Dieppe were now waiting in great numbers.

What followed was a disaster as the Germans unleashed a withering fire from cliff tops and port-side hotels. A Canadian war correspondent described the scene as men tried to disembark from their landing craft: the soldiers 'plunged into about two feet of water and machine-gun bullets laced into them. Bodies piled up on the ramp.' Neutralised by German fighters, support overhead from squadrons of RAF planes proved ineffectual. Only 29 tanks managed to make it ashore where they struggled on the shingle beach, and of those only fifteen were able to advance as far as the sea wall only to be prevented from encroaching into the town by concrete barriers.

The Dieppe Raid, which had lasted just six hours, was a costly affair – sixty percent of ground troops were killed, wounded or taken prisoner. The operation left 1,027 dead, of whom 907 were Canadian. A further 2,340 troops were captured, and one hundred and six aircraft shot down. An American, Lieutenant Edward V Loustalot, earned the unenviable distinction of becoming the first US soldier killed in wartime Europe.

Lessons learned

Despite the failure of Dieppe and the high rate of losses, important lessons were learned – that a direct assault on a well-defended harbour was not an option for any future attack; and that superiority of the air was a prerequisite. Churchill concluded that the raid had provided a 'mine of experience'. In charge of the operation, Vice Admiral Lord Louis Mountbatten, cousin to King George VI, would later say, 'If I had the same decision to make again, I would do as I did before ... For every soldier who died at Dieppe, ten were saved on D-Day.' Hitler too felt as if a lesson had been learned. Knowing that at some point the Allies would try again, he said, 'We must reckon with a totally different mode of attack and in quite a different place'.

Canadian prisoners of war being lead through Dieppe by German soldiers.

The attack would come almost two years later – 6 June 1944.

2 February 1943
The Germans Surrender at the Battle of
Stalingrad

On 2 February 1943, in what is considered *the* turning point of the Second World War in Europe, the final remnants of the German Sixth Army surrendered at the Battle of Stalingrad, perhaps the bloodiest, fiercest battle ever fought.

Stalin's City

The city, originally called Tsaritsyn, was renamed Stalingrad, Stalin's city, in April 1925, in recognition of Joseph Stalin's leading role in saving the city from the counterrevolutionary 'Whites' during the Russian Civil War. (The fact that Leon Trotsky was more instrumental in saving Tsaritsyn was quietly forgotten). Considered important because of its supply of oil, the symbolic significance of Stalingrad, bearing the name of the Soviet leader, soon outweighed its strategic importance.

Not One Step Back

The Germans started their attack on Stalingrad, Operation Blue, on 28 June 1942. Led by the Sixth Army, Germany's largest wartime army commanded by General Friedrich Paulus, the Germans were fully expecting a total victory as they pushed the Soviet forces back.

Friedrich Paulus, June 1942. German Federal Archives.

The swift German advance alarmed Stalin so much, he issued his infamous 'Not One Step Back' directive of 28 July, ordering execution for the slightest sign of defeatism. Behind the Soviet frontlines roamed a second Soviet line ready to shoot any retreating 'cowards' or 'traitors of the Motherland'. As Georgy Zhukov, one of Stalin's top generals, said, 'In the Red Army it takes a very brave man to be a coward'.

By 23 August, the German advance had reached the outskirts of Stalingrad and, with 600 planes, unleashed a devastating aerial bombardment. Entering the city, the Germans, along with their Axis comrades, comprising of Italians, Romanians and Hungarians, fought the Soviets street for street, house for house, sometimes room for room. This, as the Germans called it, was rat warfare, where a strategic stronghold changed sides so many times people lost count, where the front lines were so close one could throw back a grenade before it exploded, where snipers took their toll on the enemy, and where a soldier's life expectancy was three days – if lucky.

Stalin charged Zhukov to defend the city and formulate a plan to repulse the invader. (It's worth noting here the difference between Stalin and Hitler as military leaders. After a series of blunders earlier in the war, Stalin, although he always like to take the credit, learnt to defer and listen to the experts, men like Zhukov. Hitler however always insisted he knew best and only canvassed the opinion of others if they agreed with him.)

On 19 November 1942, the Soviet Red Army launched Zhukov's meticulously-planned counteroffensive, attacking and sweeping in from two separate directions, a pincer movement. Within four days, the two-pronged Soviet attack had met in the middle and had totally encircled the beleaguered German forces. Their objective was achieved so quickly that the Soviet film crews missed the moment, and battalions of soldiers had to re-enact the essential scenes for the benefit of the cameras.

German soldiers on the streets of Stalingrad, October 1942.
German Federal Archives.

The Soviets squeezed the 250,000 Germans and their Axis comrades tighter and tighter. As the feared Russian winter set in and temperatures dropped to the minus forties, starvation, frostbite, disease and suicide decimated the Germans. Medical facilities were, at best, crude.

Unshakeable confidence

On Christmas Day 1942, with the temperature at −25 degrees Fahrenheit, Paulus received a message from Hitler: *'You should enter the New Year with the unshakeable confidence that I and the whole of the German* Wehrmacht *will do everything in our power to relieve the defenders of Stalingrad.'*

Whether Paulus and his staff believed it and took any comfort from Hitler's promise is doubtful. Either way reinforcements, although sent, were easily repulsed and the already hideous conditions only got worse. As one

German officer put it, Stalingrad had become a 'mass grave of the *Wehrmacht*'. Even the cats and dogs had fled the city. But the Germans refused, at this point, to surrender for fear they'd be executed by the Russians.

A few German planes did manage to land within the city and were able to get troops out amidst scenes of panic, with hundreds of men fighting for the few remaining places whilst being shot at by the Soviets. (On one of the last flights out, Paulus sent his wedding ring back to his wife. He hadn't seen her since mid-1942 and would never see her again. She died in 1949).

Hitler continued to dictate strategy from far away in East Prussia with no sense of the reality on the ground, and sacking generals whose opinion differed from his. As one general recalled, 'The Fuhrer used to move his hands in big sweeps over the map – "Push here, push there". It was all vague and regardless of practical difficulties.'

Hermann Goring, his chief of the Luftwaffe, the German air force, promised Hitler that his planes could drop five hundred tons of supplies each day into Stalingrad. But with Soviet anti-aircraft guns and poor weather against them, only a fraction, perhaps up to ten percent, got through. The starving Germans resorted to eating rats and raw horseflesh. One German infantryman wrote in his diary, 'The horses have already been eaten. I would eat a cat; they say its meat is tasty. The soldiers look like corpses or lunatics. They no longer take cover from Russian shells; they haven't the strength to walk, run away and hide'. Frozen German corpses were piled up and used as sandbags.

Surrender

On 24 January, Paulus requested permission to surrender: *'Troops without ammunition or food. Effective command no longer possible. 18,000 wounded without any supplies or dressings or drugs. Further defence senseless. Collapse inevitable. Army requests immediate permission to surrender in order to save lives of remaining troops.'*

Hitler refused, saying it was the Sixth Army's historic duty to stand firm to the 'last man'.

The same day, Goring, equally as ignorant as his boss of the true situation, waxed lyrical: 'A thousand years hence Germans will speak of this battle with reverence and awe, and will remember that in spite of everything Germany's ultimate victory was decided there.'

By 26 January 1943, however, the Sixth Army was trapped within two small pockets of the city. Despite the hopeless situation, Hitler still forbade surrender. On the 30th, the tenth anniversary of his coming to power, Hitler promoted Paulus to the rank of field marshal on account that no German field marshal had ever surrendered. The following day, however, Paulus did.

Hitler, 1,000 miles away, was furious. Paulus, he shouted, *'could have freed himself from all sorrow and ascended into eternity and national immortality, but he prefers to go to Moscow … What is life? Life is the Nation. The individual must die anyway … What hurts me most, personally, is that I still promoted him to field marshal. I wanted to give him this final satisfaction. That's the last field marshal I shall appoint in this war.'*

As a Catholic, however, 'honourable' suicide was not an option for Paulus. Later, during captivity, he explained 'I [had] no intention of shooting myself for this Bohemian corporal' (referring to Hitler's highest army rank during the First World War).

A demoralised German soldier surrenders at Stalingrad, January 1943. German Federal Archives.

Two days after Paulus' surrender, on 2 February 1943, the remnants of his stricken army also surrendered; the Battle of Stalingrad was lost.

Over a million soldiers on all sides had died in the city; over 90,000 Axis troops were taken prisoner of war, including, much to Stalin's delight, twenty-two German generals, many later paraded through the streets of Moscow. Up to half the prisoners died on the marches to the Soviet prisoner-of-war camps, and most of the other half died in captivity; only about 6,000 returned home on their eventual release in 1955; about six percent of those captured during the battle of Stalingrad.

The Captive Field-Marshal

Friedrich Paulus was the Soviet Union's highest-ranking capture of the war. Later, during 1943, the Germans offered a swap – Paulus for Yakov Dzhugashvili, Stalin's son. (Stalin's real name was Dzhugashvili). Yakov had been serving as a lieutenant in the Red Army artillery when, on 16 July 1941, within a month of the Nazi invasion of the Soviet Union, he was captured by the Germans and taken prisoner. Stalin considered all prisoners as traitors to the motherland and those that surrendered he demonised as 'malicious deserters'. 'There are no prisoners of war,' he once said, 'only traitors to their homeland'. So, in response to the German offer, Paulus for his son, Stalin refused.

Following the failed assassination attempt on Hitler on 20 July 1944, Paulus, still a prisoner-of-war, became a leading opponent of Hitler's Germany, even going so far as to join the German anti-Nazi organization, the 'National Committee for a Free Germany'. Based in the Soviet Union, it called on Germans to desert Hitler for the sake of Germany's future and survival.

Post-war, Paulus appeared as a witness for the prosecution at the Nuremberg Trials. After ten years of captivity, he was released in 1953, and settled in the East German city of Dresden, where he died 1 February 1957, aged sixty-six.

The Battle of the Atlantic

The Battle of the Atlantic was the longest continuous military campaign in World War Two.

The war at sea began immediately in September 1939 with the Germans sinking merchant ships in the Indian Ocean and the South Atlantic. On 13 December 1939, the Battle of River Plate in the South Atlantic took place. The German battleship *Graf Spee* attacked a squadron of British ships off the coast of Uruguay but in doing so was damaged herself. Hitler ordered her captain, Hans Langsdorff, to scuttle the ship rather than let her fall into enemy hands. Langsdorff followed his orders and the *Graf Spee* was sunk. A week later, Langsdorff, draped in the German flag, shot himself.

The U-boat peril

In his memoirs, Winston Churchill later confessed: "The only thing that ever really frightened me during the war was the U-boat peril." Britain depended heavily on imports – from iron ore and fuel to almost seventy percent of all her food. Convoys of merchant ships crossing the Atlantic were escorted by the Royal Navy and, as far as it could reach, the RAF. But there was only so far the planes could travel, leaving a 'mid-Atlantic gap" where the convoys were particularly vulnerable to German submarines, or U-boats, which hunted in groups or 'wolf packs'.

On 9 May 1941, a British destroyer attacked a U-boat, and a boarding party managed to capture the German navy (Kriegsmarine)'s full-scale Enigma coding machine and code books. Although Bletchley Park was already having some success at deciphering the codes, they were now able to do so at will and re-route the convoys in order to avoid the wolf packs. Subsequently, within two months British losses at sea fell by eighty percent. The cracking of the Enigma code helped the Allies throughout the war in all operations.

Sink the *Bismarck*

The champion of U-boats was Commodore Karl Donitz but his superior, Admiral Erich Raeder, advocated the use of large warships. In May 1941, the Kriegsmarine's greatest warship, the *Bismarck*, one sixth of a mile long, pitted its strength against the equally impressive HMS *Hood*, the pride of the British fleet. On the 24th, exchanging fire from thirteen miles' distance, the *Hood* was sunk, losing all but three of its 1,400 crew. The *Bismarck* had been damaged but, despite leaking oil, managed to escape the British light cruisers following her. However, Bletchley Park intercepted the *Bismarck*'s codes and knew of her destination – Brest, on the western coast of France – where a fleet of British destroyers sought her out and, on

27 May, sunk her. Raeder and his warships fell from Hitler's favour and it became the turn of Donitz and his U-boats.

From August 1941, British merchant convoys started delivering supplies to the Soviet Union from bases in Scotland and Iceland. A seventeen-day journey, the Arctic Convoys were fraught with danger, not just from the Kriegsmarine and the Luftwaffe but the treacherous weather and freezing conditions. However, the convoys' contribution to the Soviet war effort, supplying tanks and guns as well as raw materials, was invaluable in the fight against Hitler.

Iron Coffins

During 1943, the British managed to breach the 'mid-Atlantic gap' with the introduction of 'Very Long-Range Liberators' and with Portugal allowing the use of its airbases in the Azores. Once the US had entered the war, America was launching more ships than the U-boats could sink and destroying more U-boats than Germany could replace. The RAF was by now successfully destroying U-boats with the aid of radar, and bombing shipyards and docks within Germany. With the Enigma decoding technology still playing its part and with three-quarters of U-boat crewmen being killed in action, the once menacing U-boat had become an 'iron coffin'. Although U-boats continued to be employed throughout the war, the 'Battle of the Atlantic', as Churchill coined it, had been won. From mid-1943, the Kriegsmarine's role was not so much offensive, as defensive, protecting German-occupied European coasts from the Allied attack they knew, one day, would come.

Yakov Stalin

Born 18 March 1907, Yakov Stalin (or Dzhugashvili) was the son of Joseph Stalin and Stalin's first wife, **Ekaterina Svanidze**. Stalin certainly didn't harbour particularly warm feelings for his son. Deprived of his father's affections and upset by a failed romance, Yakov, or Yasha as Stalin called him, once tried to shoot himself. As he lay bleeding, his father scathingly remarked, 'He can't even shoot straight'.

Yakov Stalin joined the Red Army at the outbreak of war in the East in June 1941, serving as a lieutenant in the artillery. On the first day of the war, his father told him to 'Go and fight'.

Peace-loving and gentle

His half-sister, **Svetlana Alliluyeva**, the daughter of Stalin and his second wife, **Nadezhda**, claimed in her book, *Twenty Letters to a Friend*, that Yakov never 'took any advantage [as a soldier]; never made even the slightest attempt to avoid danger... Since my father, moreover, hadn't any use for him and everybody knew it, no one in the higher echelons of the army gave him special treatment.' Yakov, according to Svetlana, was 'peace-loving, gentle and extremely quiet.' But he wasn't fond of his half brother **Vasily** (Svetlana's brother) and disliked his 'penchant for profanity', and once turned on Vasily with his fists 'like a lion'.

On 16 July, within a month of the **Nazi invasion** of the Soviet Union, Yakov was captured and taken prisoner. Stalin considered all prisoners as traitors to the motherland and those that surrendered he demonised as 'malicious deserters'. 'There are no prisoners of war,' he once said, 'only traitors to their homeland'.

Certainly Yakov, by all accounts, felt that he had failed his father. Under interrogation, he admitted that he had tried to shoot himself. His father probably would have preferred it if he had.

Stick your bayonets in the earth

Families of PoWs, or deserters, faced the harshest consequences for the failings of their sons or husbands – arrested and exiled. Yakov may have been Stalin's son but his family was not to be spared. He was married to a Jewish girl, Julia. Stalin had managed to overcome his innate anti-Semitism and grew to be quite fond of his daughter-in-law. Nonetheless, following Yakov's capture, Julia was arrested, separated from her three-year-old daughter and sent to the gulag. After two years, Stalin sanctioned her release but she remained forever traumatised by the experience.

The Germans attempted to win over Yakov, offering to introduce him to **Hermann Goring** – but he remained steadfast and refused to co-operate. But although the Germans were unable to recruit Stalin's son they still made propaganda capital out of him, dropping leaflets in the Soviet Union that claimed that the Great Leader's son had surrendered and was feeling 'alive and well'. 'Follow the example of Stalin's son', the Germans urged Soviet soldiers, 'stick your bayonets in the earth'.

Yakov was placed in a more spacious hut than others within the camp and shared a bedroom with the nephew of Vyacheslav Molotov, the Soviet Foreign Minister. In the adjoining bedroom were four British POWs, and the atmosphere between them all was strained. Yakov taunted the Brits for standing to attention when spoken to by the German officers, implying that they were cowards, and calling the British people as a whole 'Hitler's puppets'. One of the British prisoners was an Irishman, Red Cushing, who described his time as a POW with Yakov Stalin in an interview with the *Sunday Times* in 1980.

A Marshal for a Lieutenant

In 1943, Stalin was offered the chance to have his son back. The **Germans had been defeated at Stalingrad** and their Field Marshal, Friedrich Paulus, was taken prisoner by the Soviets, their highest-ranking capture of the war. The Germans offered a swap – Paulus for Yakov. Stalin refused, saying, 'I will not trade a marshal for a lieutenant'. As harsh it may seem, Stalin's reasoning did contain a logic – why should his son be freed when the sons of other Soviet families suffered – 'what would other fathers say?' asked Stalin.

Death

On 14 April 1943, the thirty-six-year-old Yakov Stalin died. The Germans maintained they shot him while he was trying to escape. They released a photograph showing his bullet-riddled body caught in barbed wire.

But it is more likely that Yakov committed suicide by throwing himself onto the electric fence. After two years of incarceration and deprivation, the news of the Katyn massacre, and his father's responsibility for it, weighed heavily on Yakov's conscience. Stalin had ordered the murder of 15,000 Polish officers in the woods of Katyn in

May 1940. The discovery of the mass grave in March 1943 was heavily publicised by the Germans. Yakov, who had befriended Polish inmates, was distraught by the news. 'Look what you bastards did to these men. What kind of people are you?' said a German officer to him.

But it was an argument over toilets, according to Red Cushing, that was the final straw. Insults and fists were thrown. Then, said Cushing, 'I saw Yakov running about as if he were insane. He just ran straight onto the wire. There was a huge flash and all the searchlights suddenly went on. I knew that was the end of him.'

5 July 1943
The Battle of Kursk

The Battle of Kursk, Germany's last grand offensive on the Eastern Front and the largest ever tank battle the world's ever seen, began 5 July 1943.

The industrial city of Kursk, 320 miles south of Moscow, had been captured by the Germans in November 1941, during the early stages of the Nazi-Soviet war, and retaken by the Soviets in February 1943. Now held by the Soviets, Kursk and the surrounding area comprised a salient, or a 'bulge', one hundred and fifty miles wide and a hundred miles deep, into German-held territory.

'My stomach turns over'

German Field-Marshall Erich von Manstein wanted to recapture Kursk as early as March 1943 by 'pinching the salient' from the north and south, thereby cutting it off from the rest of the Soviet territory. 'Operation Citadel' would also provide, argued Manstein, an immediate morale booster following the German humiliation suffered at Stalingrad, but Hitler wanted to have a new generation of tanks ready before doing so. The normally bellicose Hitler was unusually nervous about the planned offensive, confessing to his general, Heinz Guderian, 'Whenever I think of this attack, my stomach turns over'. Three times he delayed the date of attack. The delays were to prove fatal.

Intelligence had forewarned the Soviets of Nazi intentions and coupled with the delays on Hitler's part, by the time the Germans did launch their counterattack, starting at 3 am on 4 July 1943, Kursk was fully fortified and prepared. One German soldier, on the eve of the attack, thought the mission suicidal, writing bleakly, 'It is time to write out the last will and testament'. Almost a million men, 2,000 German tanks and supporting aircraft attacking, as originally planned, from north and south of the salient, were more than matched by the Soviets.

'Furious hail of bombs and shells'

The Soviets had built a line of defence up to two hundred miles deep, stretching over 3,800 miles. Hundreds of anti-tank guns were put in place, half a million mines were laid in the first trench alone – the equivalent to two mines per German soldier. 1.3 million men were waiting on the Soviet side, a further million in reserve. Leading the defence at the Battle of Kursk was Stalin's top commander, Georgi Zhukov, defender of Moscow and Leningrad. As the Red Army let ripped its barrage on the German lines, even Zhukov felt a degree of pity for the enemy 'hiding in holes, pressed to the earth to escape from the furious hail of bombs and shells'.

The Germans' hope for a blitzkrieg victory, which depended on the element of surprise, had already evaporated with Hitler's dithering, and as the Russians held out and engaged the Germans into a war of attrition, greatly favouring the Soviets, any hope of a German victory soon faded. Instead of blitzkrieg, the German soldier found himself fighting hand-to-hand, trench-by-trench. It was akin to the fighting of the First World War. Initial German gains, modest as they were, were soon lost as the Soviets counterattacked. The closest the two German attacks, north and south, got to one another was forty miles.

Prokhorovka

The climax of the Battle of Kursk took place near a village called Prokhorovka on 12 July, when one thousand tanks and a thousand aircraft on each side clashed on a two-mile front, fighting each other to a standstill. The melee was intense as tanks bumped into each other, the German tanks liable to burst into flames as their engines overheated. The Battle of Kursk dragged on for another month but with the German lines continuously disrupted by partisan activity and the Russian capacity of putting unending supplies of men and equipment into the fray, the Germans ran out of energy and resources.

Losses on both sides were huge (70,000 Germans and probably an equal if not greater number of Soviets) but with the Soviet Union's vast resource of manpower and with huge amounts of aid coming in from the US, Stalin could sustain his losses. Hitler, however, could not. Germany never again launched an offensive in the East.

Hitler, on hearing that the Western Allies had landed in Sicily, ordered a withdrawal. The Battle of Kursk came to an end on 23 August 1943.

Meanwhile, the Soviet march west had begun.

12 September 1943
The Rescue of Mussolini

On 12 September 1943, in an audacious expedition, the Italian fascist dictator, Benito Mussolini, was rescued from imprisonment by a group of German commandoes.

Background

The war was not going well for Italy and Mussolini. Campaigns against Greece and Albania had ended in ignoble defeat and things were going poorly for Italian forces fighting in North Africa. The Italian people were beginning to taste the bitter fruit of disillusionment with their leader.

On 20 January 1943, Mussolini had a meeting with his foreign minister, Galeazzo Ciano, who was also his son-in-law. Believing the war to be a lost cause, Ciano urged Mussolini to seek terms with the Allies. Mussolini flatly refused. (Indeed, Ciano had approached his British counterpart, Anthony Eden, the previous November but had no joy. Ciano had been dubious about Italy's participation in the war from the start. When, on 10 June 1940, Mussolini declared war on France, Ciano wrote in his diary, 'I am sad, very sad. The adventure begins. May God help Italy!') Ciano paid for his lack of faith when, on 5 February 1943, his father-in-law sacked him from his post. Ciano took up a post within the Vatican who were also holding discussions with the Allies into the make-up of a potential non-fascist Italian government.

The end in sight

Allied troops landed on Sicily on 10 July 1943, where they enjoyed an ecstatic welcome from the islanders. By mid-August the German forces escaped the island by crossing over the narrow Strait of Messina onto the Italian mainland. Mussolini appealed to his ally, Adolf Hitler, to send reinforcements but with German forces tied up on the Eastern Front, where they had just lost the crucial Battle of Stalingrad, no help was forthcoming.

On 19 July, Allied bombers pounded Rome, killing over a thousand civilians. Further evidence for the Italian population that defeat was inevitable.

As a result of the invasion of Sicily and the critical situation now facing Italy, Mussolini agreed to convene a meeting of the Fascist Grand Council, the first meeting since 1939. Lasting from five p.m. to three a.m. on 24 July 1943, the meeting centred around the resolution, put forward by Dino Grandi, another of Mussolini's former foreign ministers, that Mussolini be disposed and that the king, Victor Emmanuel III, should replace the dictator as head of the armed forces. Mussolini delivered an impassioned two-hour speech, exhorting his fellow fascists to put up a fight. His plea fell on deaf ears and after ten hours of heated discussion, the council voted 19 to 8 (with three abstentions) in favour of Grandi's resolution. One of those who voted against Mussolini was Galeazzo Ciano.

The most hated man in Italy

The following day, Mussolini kept his fortnightly meeting with the king, believing that the vote the previous evening was neither constitutional nor binding. He was much mistaken. Almost apologetically, Victor Emmanuel dismissed the fifty-nine-year-old dictator: 'My dear Duce, it's no longer any good. Italy has gone to bits… The soldiers don't want to fight any more… At this moment you are the most hated man in Italy.'

Mussolini was immediately arrested and imprisoned. His successor, Pietro Badoglio, appointed a new cabinet which, pointedly, contained no fascists. The Italian population rejoiced.

On 8 September, as the Allies advanced onto the mainland, Italy swapped sides and joined the Allies and, on 13 October 1943, declared war on Germany. The king and his government fled Rome and abandoned the northern half of the country to the Germans.

Meanwhile, Mussolini was kept under house arrest and frequently moved in order to keep his whereabouts hidden. On 26 August, he was moved into the Campo Imperatore Hotel, part of a ski resort high up on the mountains of Gran Sasso in the Abruzzo region of central Italy. It was here, on 12 September, that Mussolini was dramatically rescued.

Gran Sasso

The hotel had been emptied of guests. Mussolini, although complaining of stomach pains, idled away his time in relative luxury attended to by his guards, who tended to treat him more as a guest than a captive.

Meanwhile, on 26 July, Hitler had personally charged thirty-five-year-old Waffen *SS* colonel, Otto Skorzeny, an Austrian with an Action Man-type duelling scar down his left cheek, to rescue 'Italy's greatest son'. First Skorzeny (pictured below) had to find out where Mussolini was being held. Heinrich Himmler, Hitler's head of the SS, allegedly consulted astrologers to help him in the task. Instead, the more traditional method of intercepting coded radio messages revealed the exact location.

But how to rescue the man proved more challenging. The hotel, being on a mountainside, made the possibility of a parachute drop impractical. Aerial reconnaissance revealed a small field behind the hotel, so Skorzeny decided on landing a group of handpicked commandoes by glider – a risky venture but the only option available to him.

In the early afternoon of 12 September 1943, as the twelve gliders prepared to descend, Skorzeny realized that the field was not flat, as he believed, but a steep hillside. They had no choice but to crash-land on the uneven but flatter ground in front of the hotel. One glider crashed, resulting in a few injuries, but otherwise the risk paid off.

Despite being outnumbered by two hundred Italian guards, or *carabinieri*, Skorzeny's men quickly took control of the situation, forcing the *carabinieri* to surrender without a single shot being fired. Skorzeny was helped by having brought with him an Italian general, Fernando Soleti, who emerged from the glider shouting, 'Don't shoot' and sowing confusion among the Italian guards. Skorzeny attacked the radio operator with the butt of his rifle, then smashed the radio, before rushing up the stairs. Having found Mussolini's room, Skorzeny burst in announcing, 'Duce, the Fuhrer has sent me! You're free!' Overwhelmed, Mussolini, who had watched the gliders land from his window, responded, 'I knew my friend Adolf wouldn't desert me.'

Skorzeny then radioed for assistance from a small STOL (Short Take-Off and Landing) aircraft waiting nearby. The plane landed on the dangerously short and rocky field while Mussolini thanked his captors and, grinning, posed for photographs.

Skorzeny escorted Mussolini to the plane. Taking off from the plateau would be no less risky than landing. Skorzeny made what was already a dangerous undertaking even more so by insisting on joining Mussolini and the pilot in a plane designed only for two. But Skorzeny knew that if the mission failed Hitler would never forgive him and he would be forced into taking his own life. (A fate that befell Erwin Rommel a year later). With the three men on board, the pilot revved the engine to full power while twelve Germans held the plane back by its wings. On the given signal, they let go and the plane took off. But, failing to gather enough height, one of its wheels hit a rock. The plane veered off the plateau and downwards into the valley below.

The Germans leaned over the plateau and watched horrified as the plane descended but then the pilot was able to pull the aircraft up, and off it went. Meanwhile, the remaining commandos made their escape on foot. (The account is based mainly on Skorzeny's testimony which, of course, could have been and probably was exaggerated. Another witness later said that Skorzeny did not want to be in the front glider and only appeared on the scene first because the first glider had crashed, and that it was Soleti, the Italian general, that persuaded the *carabinieri* to surrender without a fight).

The plane taking Mussolini to freedom landed on an airstrip near Rome, where he was transferred onto another plane and flown to Vienna. The following day, he was flown to Munich where he was reunited with his wife, Rachele, and daughter, Edda, wife of Ciano. Two days later, he met with Hitler at the Führer's Wolf Lair HQ near Rastenburg on the Eastern Front.

Little more than a corpse

On Hitler's orders, Mussolini was returned to German-occupied northern Italy as the puppet head of a fascist republic based in the town of Salo on Lake Garda. There, having established the Italian Social Republic (ISR) with its own flag, he dealt with his son-in-law and other 'traitors' who had voted against him at the Fascist Grand Council meeting in July. Ciano had gone to Germany only to be forced back to Mussolini's new republic. Despite Edda's pleas, Mussolini had Ciano and five colleagues tried in Verona in January 1944, and five, including Ciano, were executed by firing squad on the 11 January. To add to the humiliation, they were tied to chairs and shot in the back. Ciano's last words were 'Long live Italy!' (Ciano had kept a detailed diary of his meetings with political figures, including Mussolini and Hitler. Edda, knowing the content could be embarrassing to the Nazi regime, tried to trade them in return for her husband. She failed. Two days before her husband's execution, Edda escaped to Switzerland, taking the diaries with her. They were published in 1946. Her son, Fabrizio, later wrote a book with the wonderful title, *When Grandpa Had Daddy Shot*).

Mussolini didn't have long to enjoy his new-found freedom, knowing he was no more than a puppet and that his end was nigh. In January 1945, he gave an interview in which he said: '*Seven years ago, I was an interesting person. Now, I am little more than a corpse… Yes, madam, I am finished. My star has fallen. I have no fight left in me. I work and I try, yet know that all is but a farce…. I await the end of the tragedy and — strangely detached from everything — I do not feel any more an actor. I feel I am the last of spectators.*'

Nineteen months after his rescue, Mussolini, his mistress, Clara Petacci, and a few followers attempted to escape into Switzerland. Stopped by Italian partisans, Mussolini's attempts to disguise himself with a Luftwaffe overcoat and helmet failed, and on 28 April 1945, at Lake Como in Lombardy, Mussolini and Petacci were shot. Their bodies were transported to Milan where they were beaten and urinated upon and finally left to hang upside down for public display.

28 April 1944
Exercise Tiger

As D-Day approached, training intensified. Troops were told only what they needed to know; they certainly had no idea about when or where they'd be going into action. Troops trained embarking and disembarking from landing craft. (The flat-bottomed Landing Craft, Assault vessels (LCA) weighed ten tons each, could carry thirty-eight men and travel up to ten knots per hour, while the much larger Landing Ship, Tank, LST, carried three hundred men and sixty tanks. Both vessels could sail right onto a beach.)

Exercise Tiger

It was at one such training exercise, one that involved the use of live ammunition, that tragedy struck. 23,000 American troops, the entire invading force of Utah beach, and three hundred vessels were rehearsing on Slapton Sands in South Devon on 27 and 28 April 1944 in an exercise codenamed Tiger designed to acclimatize troops as accurately as possible to what they could expect at Utah during the real thing, right down to a number of pretend dead bodies strewn around. Six villages in the area had seen the evacuation of their 3,000 inhabitants. They'd been told they would, one day, be allowed back. But when, no one knew.

30,000 acres of land around Slapton Sands, chosen because of its similarities to the intended target area of Utah beach, had been sealed off with barbed wire and sentries. On the 27th, during Exercise Tiger, poor communication resulted in a number of troops being fired upon by their own ships.

28 April 1944

The following day, even greater casualties occurred when a patrol of nine German torpedo boats bumped into a convoy of American landing craft, LSTs, quite by accident. The convoy was being escorted by a British corvette (a small warship specifically designed for escort duties) but the main escort, a destroyer, had been involved in a collision the day before and was temporarily out of action while receiving repairs in Plymouth. At 01.30, The German patrol began firing on the LSTs. Some of the American soldiers mistook the German attack for part of the exercise. Many troops, aboard LSTs, having not been instructed on how to fasten their inflatable life jackets, and laden down in full battle dress, drowned. Fuel caught fire and many men suffered terrible burns. Between the two events, 946 servicemen were killed and some two hundred wounded.

Aftermath

The tragedy of Exercise Tiger was kept hidden, the dead swiftly buried, and survivors sworn to secrecy, lest it should damage morale. Doctors, treating the wounded, were told to ask no questions. The full extent of the disaster was not fully known until the 1970s. Ten of those declared missing, presumably dead, were of high enough rank to be carrying highly secret instructions and plans. The commanders feared that some of these men might have been picked up by the Germans and taken prisoner. Had such a scenario manifested, the whole D-Day operation would have been in serious jeopardy. Much to all-round relief, divers accounted for all ten corpses.

On D-Day itself, 6 June 1944, 23,250 US troops landed in France via Utah beach for the cost of 210 men killed or wounded, considerably less than the casualties sustained during Exercise Tiger exercise on Slapton Sands.

6 June 1944
D-Day and Omaha beach

D-Day, 6 June 1944, a date that altered the course of history, saw the largest amphibious invasion ever launched. Led by troops from the US, Great Britain and Canada, and involving Allied divisions from across the globe, the invasion of Occupied France, codenamed Operation Overlord, had been years in the planning and subject to the utmost secrecy.

Five beaches

The Americans, it was decided, would land on the two western beaches in Normandy, codenamed Utah and Omaha; while the British would attack via the middle and eastern beaches, codenamed Gold and Sword; and between these two, the Canadians would land at Juno.

At 5.50, on 6 June, the 1,738th day of the war, 138 Allied ships, positioned between three and thirteen miles out, began their tremendous bombardment of the German coastal defences. Above them, one thousand RAF bombers attacked, followed in turn by one thousand planes of the USAAF. Between them, the aircrews flew 13,688 sorties over the course of D-Day alone.

From their ships, soldiers, weighed down with weapons and seventy pounds of equipment, scaled down scramble nets and into their flat-bottomed landing craft. It took over three hours for the vessels to traverse the eleven or so miles to the coast. The men, trembling with abject fear, shivering from the cold and suffering from severe seasickness, endured and held on as their tightly-packed vessels were buffeted by six-foot high waves and eighteen-miles per hour winds. At 6.30, the first US troops landed on Omaha and Utah beaches.

On all five landing spots, the most dangerous task fell to the men whose task it was to explode and neutralise the German mines littered across the beaches in order to clear a path for the first full wave of troops coming up directly behind them. The courage to attempt such a task is beyond imagination. The fatality rate was horrendously high, reaching seventy-five percent.

Omaha Beach

The defences around Omaha were formidable. Erwin Rommel's men had placed thousands of 'dragon's teeth' on the beach, designed to take out the base of landing craft, and topped with mines. Gun emplacements had the entire length of beach within their range. The naval bombardment and subsequent aerial bombardment although effective elsewhere had made little impact on Omaha. Ten landing craft were sunk. Men, leaping into water too deep, drowned, weighed down by their equipment.

The US soldiers, led by General Omar Bradley, facing the strongest and most experienced German troops from the 352nd Infantry Division, jumped from their landing craft into a barrage of gunfire. All but two of their specially-built swimming tanks were sunk, their crews trapped inside, depriving the advancing Americans covering fire. With Omaha beach offering little in the way of shelter or protection, casualties among the Americans were appallingly high. Many returned to the freezing waters and floated on their backs, keeping their noses above the waterline.

Among the second wave, landing an hour later, was photographer Robert Capa (pictured below). Under relentless fire, Capa managed to take one hundred and six pictures. (On returning to the *Life* offices in London with the unprocessed films, a laboratory assistant accidentally destroyed all but eleven of Capa's photographs).

The congested beach at Omaha had become a killing field, littered with bodies, burning tanks and equipment. The noise of screams, gunfire and bombardment filled the air. Terrified men, sprinting as best as they could across the expanse of beach, found a degree of cover at the base of the cliffs – if they managed to get that far; many did not.

Finally, at 8 a.m., as destroyers came close enough to pound and weaken the German defences, sufficient numbers had congregated to begin the climb up the cliffs. By 11 a.m., a contingent broke out and captured the village of Vierville. Their colleagues, still pinned down on the beach and with the tide now coming in, were in danger of being pushed back to the sea. But the German soldiers, in maintaining their constant barrage, were close to exhaustion. Finally, at 2 p.m., the first beach exit was cleared. By four p.m., tanks and vehicles were able to move off the beach. By the end of the day, 34,000 troops had been landed on Omaha beach for the cost of 2,400 killed or wounded.

D-Day had begun.

Juan Pujol Garcia

Juan Pujol Garcia was unique among Second World War
agents – he was the only one to offer his services as a
double agent as opposed to all others who had been
captured and 'turned'. Bespectacled, balding and timid,
Pujol was not the image usually associated with a double
agent, let alone Britain's most effective one.

Born in Barcelona on 14 February 1912, Pujol was
working on a chicken farm when, in 1936, the Spanish
Civil War broke out. He managed to fight for both the
Republican side and the Nationalists. He was committed
to neither and hated the extreme views they each
represented. By the end of the war, he was able to claim
that he had served in both armies without firing a single
bullet for either.

He emerged from the experience with an intense
dislike for extreme ideologies and, for the 'good of
humanity', sought to help achieve a more moderate
system. With the outbreak of war in 1939, three times he
approached British services in Lisbon and Madrid, offering
to spy for them, only to be turned away without an

interview. Undeterred, Pujol decided to become a double agent. He offered his services to the German Abwehr (military intelligence) service based also in Lisbon, offering to spy on the English, claiming that as a diplomat working in London, he knew England well.

For the good of humanity

His audacity was certainly impressive – he had never visited England, nor could he speak the language, and he had forged a British passport without ever having seen a real one. Incredibly, the Germans fell for the story, put him through an intensive training course, and supplied him with the tools of the trade: invisible ink, cash, and a code name – Arabel, and sent him on assignment to England with instructions to build a network of spies.

Agent Arabel

This Pujol did. Soon, he had a team of agents working for him. They included disillusioned men and women, disaffected English nationals, and people prepared to betray Britain in return for wine. Between them, they supplied Pujol a steady stream of information which, in turn, he passed on to the Abwehr.

But it was all false. Pujol never went to England. Instead, he ensconced himself in Lisbon and armed with a Blue Guide to England and various books he found in the library, made everything up. He reported on non-existent troops, and routinely mixed up his pounds, shillings and pence. The Germans seemed not to notice. He even had the nerve to post his reports from Lisbon letterboxes, telling his German paymasters that among his agents was a pilot who regularly flew to Portugal, posting his correspondence locally.

Agent Garbo

Soon, the British were intercepting his messages and were delighted at the amount of false information being fed to the enemy. They determined to track him down. But in April 1942, Pujol approached them. This time, not surprisingly, they took his offer more seriously. Given the code name Garbo, Pujol began working with a Spanish and German-speaking Security Service officer, Tomás (Tommy) Harris.

The Germans were so impressed with the work of their Arabel and his network of agents that they rarely bothered to recruit further agents. For the British, it was imperative that the Abwehr continued to trust Arabel.

Thus, the information Pujol and Harris fed them was often accurate but of low importance, or of high value but timed so that by the time the Germans received it, it was too late to do anything.

Soon, Pujol's team of fictional agents numbered 27, each with their own backstory, supposedly based across the UK. Some were caught, imprisoned or, as Arabel told the Germans, had become untrustworthy. On one notorious occasion, a Liverpool-based agent had died. The Secret Service even had his obituary published in the local newspaper, and Arabel got the Abwehr to pay the agent's 'widow' an annual pension.

In the lead up to D-Day in June 1944, Pujol played a major role in keeping much of German strength focussed on a possible invasion at Pas-de-Calais. The difficulties the Allies had landing on Normandy, particularly via Omaha beach, would have been that much more difficult if it had not been for the efforts of Britain's Spanish double agent.

Such was Pujol's success, he was awarded an MBE by Britain's King George VI and an Iron Cross, personally authorized by Hitler (a rare event for a foreigner of the Reich). Pujol was perhaps the only individual to be so highly decorated by both sides.

Following the war, Pujol faked his death in Angola, and settled to a quiet life with his family in Venezuela. Pujol died in Caracas on 10 October 1988, aged seventy-six.

The 20 July Bomb Plot

Count Stauffenberg loses faith

A fervent supporter of Hitler, thirty-six-year-old Count Claus von Stauffenberg had fought bravely during the Second World War for the Fuhrer. Fighting in Tunisia in 1943, Stauffenberg was badly wounded, losing his left eye, his right hand and two fingers of his left. Once recovered, Stauffenberg was transferred to the Eastern Front where he witnessed the atrocities firsthand which made him question his loyalty. As it became increasingly apparent that Germany would not win the war, Stauffenberg lost faith in Hitler and the Nazi cause.

At some point in early 1944, Stauffenberg joined a group of German officers intent on bringing the war to a quick end and negotiating a peace with the Allies. Their biggest obstacle was of course Hitler.

But the plotters received a bit of luck when Stauffenberg was appointed onto the staff of the Reserve Army, reporting directly to General Friedrich Fromm, another officer who had lost faith in the Nazi cause. When Stauffenberg was invited to a meeting in Hitler's Wolf's Lair in Rastenburg, East Prussia, for 20 July, the opportunity seemed perfect.

The conspirators hatched their plan, codenamed Valkyrie, and crucial to its success was Stauffenberg's proximity to Hitler.

'I Am Alive, I Am Alive'

About to attend the meeting, Stauffenberg, lacking time to prepare two devices, only managed to prepare one bomb. With it set to detonate after ten minutes, Stauffenberg entered the meeting room at the Wolf's Lair and found Hitler poring over a large air reconnaissance report from the Eastern Front spread across a table. The Count placed his briefcase beneath the map table and, as prearranged, received a phone call, necessitating his immediate attention and departure.

Whilst Stauffenberg made good his escape, an attendant, with his foot, pushed the briefcase further under the heavy oak table so that when, at 12.42, the two pound bomb went off, the thickness of the wood spared Hitler the main thrust of the explosion.

Billows of black smoke poured from the windows of the meeting room, and staggering out leaning on each other were two men, their clothes torn to shreds, their skin blackened, and their hair singed. One of them was General Wilhelm Keitel, the other was Hitler himself, muttering "What was that? I am alive, I am alive!"

Arrest him immediately

Hitler was examined – contusion on the left arm, damage to his eardrums and wooden splinters in his legs from the floorboards. (His trousers were torn to shreds, as seen in the photograph). Considering his proximity to the bomb his survival was miraculous. So superficial his injuries he was able to keep an appointment that afternoon with Italian leader, Benito Mussolini, meeting him in person at the local railway station and shaking Il *Duce's* hand with his left. Hitler himself put his survival down to the hand of providence. Germany, the fates dictated, would win the war and Hitler's life had been spared to ensure it.

Others had been more seriously injured and taken to hospital. Four of them later died. The movements of all were scrutinised and it soon became apparent that

Stauffenberg, seen leaving hurriedly in his car, was the culprit. "Arrest him immediately!" bellowed Hitler.

Hitler is dead

Early afternoon, Thursday 20 July 1944 – Count Claus von Stauffenberg, believing that he had successfully killed Hitler, returned to Berlin. The first part of the operation had been successfully completed. Now he issued the codeword, Valkyrie, the instruction for the Reserve Army to place Germany under a state of emergency. General Friedrich Fromm, Stauffenberg's senior officer within the Reserve Army, informed local commanders that a new administration would be formed.

However, one of those commanders, Major Remer, received a telephone call directly from Hitler where the Fuhrer informed the Major that, contrary to popular rumour, he was still very much alive – and in control.

When it became obvious that the coup had failed, Fromm, in an attempt to distance himself from the conspirators, ordered the arrest and immediate execution of Stauffenberg. The Count was detained and duly shot, along with three others, at one in the morning, just over 12 hours after the bomb had gone off, and hastily buried in the grounds of the War Ministry.

Himmler takes control

But it did Fromm little good. Once Heinrich Himmler, Hitler's SS boss, had arrived in Berlin, he re-established control of the city and the mass arrests began, and among the first to be arrested was Fromm. He also ordered the exhumation of Stauffenberg's body. The Count's final resting place has since remained a mystery – *until recently*.

Many committed suicide rather than face Nazi justice. The ringleaders were rounded up and hanged by piano wire, their deaths recorded onto film and the films sent to the Wolf's Lair for Hitler to watch at his pleasure. Over the coming months more than 7,000 were arrested, of whom 4,980 were executed. Fromm remained imprisoned until 12 March 1945, when he too was shot.

Rommel's fateful choice

The highest-ranking victim of this post-July purge was one of Hitler's favourite and most-ablest generals, Erwin Rommel. Rommel, who shared the same birthday as Stauffenberg, 15 November, although not directly involved, had previously voiced sympathy for the plan. Once his endorsement came to light, he was given the option of honourable suicide or subjecting himself to the humiliation and the kangaroo court of Nazi justice, and his family deported to a concentration camp. He chose the former and, on 14 October 1944, accompanied by two generals sent by Hitler, poisoned himself. He was, as promised, buried with full military honours, his family pensioned off.

Aftermath

Those who had been at Hitler's side in the conference room on 20 July were awarded a specially-made 'Wounded Medal', either in black, silver or gold, that bore Hitler's signature and the date. It was, for the remaining months of the war, the ultimate badge of loyalty and honour.

The buildings that made up the Wolf's Lair were demolished soon after the war but today, on the site, is a memorial stone dedicated to Stauffenberg – the "bravest of the best" as Churchill described the fallen Count.

4 August 1944.
The Betrayal of Anne Frank

'I hope I shall be able to confide in you completely, as I have never been able to do in anyone before, and I hope that you will be a great support and comfort to me.'

Her voice has come to symbolise the Holocaust, one victim among the six million who spoke for them all, a testament to all who perished with her.

Anne Frank died aged fifteen in the Bergen-Belsen concentration camp in early March 1945.

Born 12 June 1929, Anne and her older sister, Margot, lived their early years in Frankfurt. But in 1933, following Hitler's appointment as Chancellor, the Franks, as a Jewish family, became concerned for their safety as the Nazis introduced increasingly fanatical anti-Semitic legislation.

The Franks Move to Amsterdam

In late 1933 Anne's father, Otto, was offered and accepted a business opportunity in Amsterdam. In February 1934 his wife and daughters joined him in the Netherlands. Of the half million Jews living in Germany in 1933, about 320,000 had emigrated by 1939.

In May 1940 Hitler launched his attack against France and the Low Countries. Rotterdam was heavily bombed and, on 15 May, the Dutch, fearing further losses, surrendered.

Occupied Netherlands

Life for the Jewish population in Nazi-occupied Netherlands became increasingly intolerable and dangerous. In July 1942, Otto Frank received an order to report his eldest daughter for a work camp. The Franks, fearing for their lives, decided they had no option but to go into hiding.

On 6 July 1942, the Franks moved into their secret annex, behind Otto's business premises at 263 Prinsengracht, and in doing so left their flat in a state of chaos to give the impression of a family on the run. The annex consisted of three floors, its entrance concealed by a large, wooden bookcase. They were to live in this self-imposed incarceration for over two years. From the outside the Franks were provided with food, provisions, news and humanity by a small group of trusted business associates of Otto's. A week after moving in, they were joined by Hermann and Auguste van Pels and their sixteen-year-old son, Peter. On 16 November, they were joined by a German dentist and veteran of the First World War, Fritz Pfeffer.

Anne and Peter had a brief flirtation, which, although pleasurable, was, for such a young girl, perplexing. For Anne, becoming aware of her sexuality but in such a confined and claustrophobic atmosphere and tainted with the lack of normality and the constant nag of fear, it must have been unbearably confusing and difficult. But there was always the solace and consolation of her diary.

The Diary

Anne had always shown a propensity to write and on her thirteenth birthday, a month before their flight, she received from her father an autograph book. With its thick blank pages, tartan cover and lock and key, Anne was delighted by her present and immediately began using it as a diary.

As with many a teenager, a diary is a constant companion and source of comfort, allowing the writer to express their feelings, their frustrations, their fears and hopes for the future, and their beliefs and changing attitudes. And so it was for Anne, an ordinary girl with an extraordinary talent, in extra-ordinary circumstances. The last entry in Anne's diary is dated 1 August 1944:

Believe me, I'd like to listen, but it doesn't work, because if I'm quiet and serious, everyone thinks I'm putting on a new act and I have to save myself with a joke, and then I'm not even talking about my own family, who assume I must be sick, stuff me with aspirins and sedatives, feel my neck and forehead to see if I have a temperature, ask about my bowel movements and berate me for being in a bad mood, until I just can't keep it up anymore, because when everybody starts hovering over me, I get cross, then sad, and finally end up turning my heart inside out, the bad part on the outside and the good part on the inside, and keep trying to find a way to become what I'd like to be and what I could be if... if only there were no other people in the world. Yours, Anne M. Frank

Three days later, 4 August, Nazi security police, led by an Austrian called Karl Josef Silberbauer, burst into the annex and arrested the Franks and their companions. They had been betrayed but by whom we will never know. The call was taken by Silberbauer's commanding officer, a SS lieutenant called Julius Dettmann, who merely said the call had come from a 'reliable source'. (Following the end of the war, Dettmann was arrested and interned as a prisoner of war. He committed suicide in July 1945). Otto Frank was giving Peter van Pels an English lesson when the Nazis entered the annex. On seeing Anne, Silberbauer said to Otto, 'You have a lovely daughter'. He couldn't believe that the Franks and their friends had been in the annex for over two years. As proof, Otto showed Silberbauer the pencil lines where he had charted Anne and Margot's growth since 1942.

Auschwitz and Bergen-Belsen

The Franks, the van Pels and Fritz Pfeffer, the German dentist, were taken to a prison in Amsterdam, then to the Westerbork transit camp, in the northeast of the country. On 3 September 1944, all eight were deported to Auschwitz-Birkenau in Poland on the last train to leave the Netherlands for the extermination camp. Immediately, on arriving at Auschwitz, Otto was separated from his wife and daughters – he never saw them again. He did, however, remain with Peter van Pels and was reunited with Pfeffer. Pfeffer died in Auschwitz on 20 December 1944 while Peter was put on a death march out of Auschwitz in January 1945 and died in Mauthausen, Austria, aged eighteen, on 5 May 1945, the very day the camp was liberated. Peter's parents both died as well, his father gassed.

In October 1944, the girls were relocated to Bergen-Belsen whilst their mother remained in Auschwitz where she was to die on 6 January 1945 from starvation.

Margot and Anne, already weak, deteriorated further and when a typhus epidemic swept through Belsen killing almost 20,000 inmates, the sisters were amongst the victims. The exact date of their deaths is not known but it was early March 1945, just weeks before the camp's liberation.

Otto Frank and his daughter's diary

Otto Frank, 1968. Dutch National Archives.

Otto, the only resident of the annex to survive, returned to Amsterdam following the war knowing that his wife was dead but unsure of his daughters' fates. He learnt, on returning home, of their deaths and received from friends Anne's diary. This man, his life devastated by cruelty and

145

inhumanity, sat down and read the secret diary of his deceased daughter.

He read of Anne's desire to be published, to be known as a writer, and decided to devote the rest of his life to Anne's work. He was to die in 1980, aged ninety-one.

The diary was first published in the Netherlands in 1947 and five years later in the US and the UK. The name Anne Frank rapidly became known throughout the world.

Seventy years later and her name lives on, and Anne's diary, recognised as a timeless classic, remains essential reading for all humanity.

16 December 1944
The Battle of the Bulge

16 December 1944 saw the start of the German 'Ardennes Offensive' (the Battle of the Bulge). It was to be the US' biggest pitched battle in their history, involving 600,000 American troops. The Allied forces were advancing towards Germany, pushing the Germans back town by town and believing the war to be almost won. But this was Hitler's last attempt to stop the momentum. His aim was to advance through the wooded area of the Ardennes in Luxembourg and Belgium and cut the Allied armies in two and then push on towards the port of Antwerp, a vital Allied stronghold.

The Allies knew there was a build-up of German troops and equipment around the Ardennes but never believed Hitler was capable of such a bold initiative. Only the day before the attack, the British commander, Bernard Montgomery, told Dwight D Eisenhower, the Allies' Supreme Commander, that the Germans would be incapable of staging 'major offensive operations'. Captured

Germans spilled the plans but their information was ignored. Thus, the attack came as a complete surprise.

'Nuts'

Thick snow and heavy fog prevented the Americans from employing their airpower and the German advance of 250,000 men forced a dent in the American line (hence battle of the 'Bulge'). Germans, dressed in American uniforms and driving captured US jeeps, caused confusion and within five days the Germans had surrounded almost 20,000 Americans at the crossroads of Bastogne. Their situation was desperate but when the German commander gave his American equivalent, Major-General Anthony McAuliffe, the chance to surrender, McAuliffe answered with just the one word – 'Nuts'.

US soldiers near the town of St Vith were not so lucky and 8,000 of them surrendered – the largest surrender of US troops since the American Civil War eighty years before. Elsewhere, the Germans taunted the Americans, using loudspeakers to ask, 'How would you like to die for Christmas?'

'Lovely weather for killing Germans'

US General George Patton appealed for divine intervention – 'Sir, this is Patton talking', he said, addressing God in a small Luxembourg church, 'You have just got to make up Your mind whose side You're on.' On Patton's urging, God must have made up His mind for near Christmas the fog lifted, and the Americans were able to launch their planes. Patton, considering the weather, said, 'It's a cold, clear Christmas – lovely weather for killing Germans'. While Patton moved reinforcements into Bastogne and relieved its desperate defenders, Montgomery prevented the Germans from crossing the River Meuse.

The Americans then counterattacked; the Germans ran out of fuel and the bulge was burst. The Ardennes Offensive did delay the Allied advance but on 22 January the Germans began their retreat and by the 28th the line was back to where it was on 16 December. But at a cost – the US lost over 80,000 men killed or wounded. Amongst the dead, were one hundred and one unarmed American prisoners, murdered by the SS. The Germans lost over 100,000 and, vitally, much of its aircraft and tanks which, at that stage of the war, were impossible to replace. The march on Berlin was back on.

The struggle and conditions at Bastogne are brought to life in the excellent US TV mini-series Band of Brothers. There is also a 1965 film starring Henry Fonda and Terry Savalas, 'The Battle of the Bulge', a classic American epic where sometimes historical accuracy takes second place to entertainment but none the worse for that!

30 January 1945
The Sinking of the *Wilhelm Gustloff*,
the Worst Maritime Disaster In History

30 January 1945 – nine hours after leaving port and seventy minutes after being hit, the huge liner, the *Wilhelm Gustloff*, slipped under the waves and sunk. A small fleet of ships and boats arrived on the scene and managed to pluck a few survivors from the icy Baltic waters and rescued many of those on the lifeboats. Over a thousand were rescued but… an estimated 9,343 people died, half of them children – six times the 1,517 that died on the *Titanic* in 1912.

The sinking of the *Wilhelm Gustloff* remains the biggest maritime disaster in history.

We have all heard of the *Titanic*. A century after that fateful night, the disaster remains within our global consciousness. Even before James Cameron's epic 1998 film, we knew of the iceberg, the 'women and children first', and the band that played on.

But how many of us have even heard of the *Wilhelm*

The Luxury Liner

The ship was named after the assassinated leader of the Swiss Nazi Party (yes, Switzerland in the 1930s had its own Nazi Party), murdered in his own home in February 1936.

Wilhelm Gustloff.

The ship, the *Wilhelm Gustloff*, weighing 25,000 tons and almost 700 feet in length, was an impressive sight, and could carry almost 2,000 passengers and crew. Launched in 1937, it began its life as a luxury cruise liner for the German workers of Hitler's Third Reich, and, until the outbreak of the Second World War, had sailed over fifty cruises.

Wartime

For the first year of the war the *Wilhelm Gustloff* served as a hospital ship before being held in dock in the port of Gotenhafen on the Baltic coast (modern-day Gdynia) where, until early 1945, it served as barracks for U-boat trainees.

Hitler had launched Operation Barbarossa, the invasion of the Soviet Union, in June 1941 and German forces had fought all the way to within sight of Moscow. But then the tide of war turned against the Nazis, and Stalin launched his own counterattack.

By October 1944, the Soviet Union's Red Army had fought the Germans out of the Soviet Union and broken through into East Prussia.

The Red Army Approaches

With the apocalyptic Red Army bearing down on them, the German civilians of East Prussia, desperate to get away, fled to the Baltic ports hoping to be evacuated out. Many of those caught in the maelstrom of the Soviet advance were murdered and raped.

The *Wilhelm Gustloff*, along with any other serviceable ship in the area, was pressed into service to aid the evacuation of German civilians. With forty-eight hours notice before departure, the scenes in frozen Gotenhafen were of panic as people, frantic for a place, fought on the dock and surged aboard the ship.

Evacuation

By the time it left, on 30 January, 10,582 people (forty percent of whom were children) had crammed onto a ship designed for less than 2,000. Of the three designated military escorts, two broke down, leaving only one torpedo boat to accompany the huge liner. The ship had four captains who argued over the best course to take – shallow or deep waters, a straight line for speed or zig-zags to help avoid detection. Poor visibility, heavy snow and freezing temperatures further hampered progress.

When the captains were informed of a German minesweeper convoy coming towards them, they decided, after much argument, to switch on the navigation lights to avoid colliding into the convoy, but by doing so the ship also became visible to a Soviet submarine lurking nearby.

Hit

The submarine fired three torpedoes, each hitting its target. The ensuing scenes of panic cannot be imagined. Most of the lifeboats had frozen onto their davits, leaving only a few that could be put into use. As the ship listed to one side, many people were trapped below decks, others crushed in the stairways, while many fell into the freezing waters. Children drowned in lifejackets too big. People fought and clubbed each other to get onto the few available lifeboats, while many jumped to their deaths.

It was, coincidentally, the birthdate of Wilhelm Gustloff, born 30 January 1895. The day the ship sunk would have been his fiftieth birthday. It was also the twelfth anniversary of Hitler coming to power.

The sinking of the *Wilhelm Gustloff* on 30 January 1945 remains the greatest maritime disaster to ever have taken place. But why, when the tragic story of the *Titanic* is so known to us, does the *Wilhelm Gustloff* remain a forgotten catastrophe?

To help answer this, I quote from historian, David F. Krawczyk. Below I paraphrase some of his observations:

1. The disaster occurred during wartime

Many view wartime disasters as less 'tragic' than those occurring during peacetime.

2. The victims were on the 'losing' side

Although the passengers were predominately civilian, they were German, and post-war sympathy for Germany was not overly forthcoming.

3. German war-guilt has repressed the disaster

A nation's war guilt and repression of memory has served to push the *Wilhelm Gustloff* into obscurity, although German writer and Nobel Prize winner, Gunter Grass, wrote of the disaster and the preceding assassination of Gustloff in his 2002 novel, *Crabwalk*.

4. Russian retribution for Nazi occupation

When the Nazis broke their pact with Stalin and invaded Soviet Russia in 1941, their tactics were often brutal. Hitler himself made it clear that this was a war different from that waged in the West, calling it a 'war of extermination'. When the tide eventually turned against Germany and the Soviets were marching towards Berlin, the Red Army showed no mercy – and exacted horrific revenge. Since the Soviets were in control of the Bay of Danzig both near the end of the war and for many years after, the Polish civilians were not allowed to mourn the loss of life on a German ship.

5. World sentiment regarding Nazi atrocities

As the world learned more about Nazi war crimes and systematic genocide, subdued global reaction to a disaster on this scale was perhaps understandable. Under other circumstances, 4,000 innocent children dying in a single disaster would certainly be mourned by almost anyone in a 'friendly' or 'enemy' nation.

6. The ship was named after a prominent Nazi leader

Wilhelm Gustloff was leader of the Nazi Party in Switzerland. David Krawczyk, on his site, wonders if the profile of the ship might have been higher if it had been named after a city or non-Nazi figure.

7. Demise of so many refugees (mostly women and children)

For months, the disaster remained largely unreported both inside and outside Germany. Inside the imploding Germany, Hitler wanted to suppress awareness about the death of so many. The Western Allies avoided it too; it would not have made for a popular news story where one of its allies had caused a disaster that had claimed the lives of so many women and children.

8. There is no American connection or Hollywood profile

Since comparisons are inevitable, we can see how the Titanic profile was raised even higher worldwide with an Academy-Award winning movie from Hollywood. Unlike the *Titanic*, the *Wilhelm Gustloff* was not sailing towards America, nor did it have any American passengers on its decks.

9. There were no rich victims on board

In another comparison to the *Titanic*, none of the *Wilhelm Gustloff* passengers on the fateful voyage were rich or of society's elite. They were simply refugees trying to escape a terrible situation.

13 February 1945
The Bombing of Dresden

From about ten p.m. on the night of 13 February 1945 until noon the following day, the East German city of Dresden was the subject of one the most intense bombing raids of the Second World War. Several German cities were targeted throughout the war but it is the bombing of Dresden, and its utter destruction, that came to symbolise the work of the RAF's Bomber Command and its commander, Sir Arthur Harris.

Florence of the Elbe

Germany's seventh largest city, 100 miles southeast of Berlin, Dresden was known as the 'Florence of the Elbe', such was its architectural splendour, its large collections of art and quaint timbered buildings. In February 1945, the city's population had been temporarily inflated by a huge influx of German refugees, perhaps up to 350,000, fleeing the Soviet advance sixty miles away to the east.

With only minimal anti-aircraft guns, few German troops, and limited war-related industry, Dresden was still deemed a legitimate target – for Arthur 'Bomber' Harris's intention was not so much military but 'moral bombing', to demoralise the civilian population and thereby shorten the war (despite evidence during the Blitz that instead of demoralising civilians, bombing only hardened resolve). The strategic objective of bombing Dresden and other cities in eastern Germany was, as agreed at the Anglo-American Yalta Conference, to help alleviate the pressures on Soviet forces advancing into Germany on the Eastern Front.

Dresden, c1900. Library of Congress.

The Allied commanders studied aerial photographs of German cities and specifically targeted areas of heavy residential populations. His aim, said Harris, was to make the 'rubble bounce'.

Thus, on Tuesday, 13 February 1945, two waves of RAF Lancaster bombers, numbering 773 in total, attacked Dresden. The following morning, 527 bombers of the USAAF (US air force) attacked with the objective of hitting the fire fighters tackling the inferno caused by the RAF the previous evening and causing even greater chaos. Of all these aircraft, only eight were shot down.

Devastation

2,640 tons of bombs were dropped on Dresden, two thirds of which were incendiary bombs. A firestorm erupted in an area eight miles square reaching temperatures of 1,500 degrees centigrade engulfing the narrow, medieval streets. Ninety percent of buildings within the city centre were destroyed, including over twenty hospitals. Smoke rose up to 15,000 feet.

Dresden had been obliterated.

The Allies knew that a bomb shelter or a cellar would only provide protection for about three hours before becoming unbearably hot and full of carbon monoxide, and so forcing the civilians back outside. Thus a second wave of bombs was dropped precisely three hours after the first batch – again to maximise the number of casualties. Many bombs were adapted so that they would explode hours after falling – the idea to cause maximum casualties against civilians who were trying to remove the devices. Air bombs were dropped with the intention of blowing off roof tiles, allowing incendiary bombs to fall unimpeded into the interior of buildings, and to blow out windows to allow greater ventilation to stoke the flames.

The RAF's Bomber Command bombing Dresden, February 1945.

People died from the lack of oxygen as the firestorm sucked the air out of the atmosphere. One witness described seeing people suddenly falling dead as if shot but, as she found later, they were dropping dead from the lack of oxygen. Many unfortunates jumped into a huge water tank hoping to escape the suffocating heat, only to find the water inside was boiling. 'Human beings were thrown to the ground or flung alive into the flames by winds which exceeded 150 mph,' wrote one witness.

The Dresden zookeeper wrote, 'The elephants gave spine-chilling screams. The baby cow elephant was lying in the narrow barrier-moat on her back, her legs up in the sky. She had suffered severe stomach injuries and could not move. A 90 cwt. cow elephant had been flung clear across the barrier moat and the fence by some terrific blast wave, and stood there trembling. I had no choice but to leave these animals to their fate.'

One witness described the city as a 'sea of flames'. Another described 'the hot wind of the firestorm (which) threw people back into the burning houses they were trying to escape from.' A labour camp inmate, a British soldier called Victor Gregg, incarcerated nearby, described the scene: 'As the incendiaries fell, the phosphorus clung to the bodies of those below, turning them into human torches. The screaming of those who were being burned alive was added to the cries of those not yet hit'.

But not all witnesses were horrified: one Jewish inmate of a German labour camp watched the sky burn bright over the city of Dresden: 'We were in heaven,' he wrote later. 'To all of us, it was absolute salvation. This was how we knew that the end (of the war) was near.'

Slaughterhouse-Five

The American novelist Kurt Vonnegut, who died in 2007, was a prisoner-of-war near Dresden, having been captured in December 1944 during the Battle of the Bulge. In the days following the raid on the city, Vonnegut and his fellow PoWs were put to work collecting bodies for burial while German civilians swore and threw stones at them. Eventually, wrote Vonnegut, 'there were too many corpses to bury. So instead the Germans sent in troops with flamethrowers. All these civilians' remains were burned to ashes.' Vonnegut's experiences in Dresden formed the backdrop of much of his work, including his most famous novel, *Slaughterhouse-Five*.

For the sake of increasing the terror

Estimates to how many died varied with the Nazis exaggerating the figure for propaganda purposes, but it is now accepted that some 25,000 lost their lives in this single raid.

Dresden destroyed, autumn 1945. Deutsche Fotothek

During the blitz, Germany's bombardment of the UK, some 60,000 civilians lost their lives. The Allied bombing of Germany caused eight times that number of deaths. For every ton of bombs dropped by the Germans during the war, the Allies dropped three hundred.

Although initially enthusiastic about the bombing raids, Winston Churchill tried to distance himself and, following Dresden, questioned Harris's methods of *'bombing German cities simply for the sake of increasing the terror … The destruction of Dresden remains a serious query against the conduct of Allied bombing … I feel the need for more precise concentration upon military objectives.'* Harris responded angrily that the attacks had been necessary in order to hasten the German surrender and diminish further allied casualties.

In 1956, Dresden was twinned with Coventry, a city that was heavily bombed several times during the early years of the war, most notably on 14 November 1940, at the height of the Blitz.

Bomber Harris

In his memoirs, *Bomber Offensive*, published 1947, Arthur Harris wrote, 'the attack on Dresden was at the time considered a military necessity by much more important people than myself.' In a televised interview from 1977, never broadcast and only rediscovered in 2013, Harris said: 'If I had to have the same time again I would do the same again, but I hope I wouldn't have to … The bombers kept over a million fit Germans out of the German army… Manning the anti-aircraft defences; making the ammunition, and doing urgent repairs, especially tradesmen.'

One story has it that one evening, during the war, Harris was driving home when he was pulled up by a policeman on a motorbike. 'Sir, you're driving much too fast, you might kill someone.' To which, Harris replied, 'It's my business to kill people – Germans.' On realising who he was talking to, the policeman apologised and gave Harris a fast escort home.

Sir Arthur Harris, 1944. Imperial War Museums.

Finally recognised

But whatever the morality of Bomber Command's work, its pilots faced a dangerous task: 55,573 British, Australian, New Zealand, Canadian and other Commonwealth pilots and crewmen lost their lives and 8,403 were wounded, a sixty percent causality rate, far higher than most other forms of armed service during the war.

Post-war, those who fought with Bomber Command and survived were dismayed and insulted to find that their efforts were not to be recognised with a campaign medal. In June 2012, seven decades on, a Bomber Command memorial was unveiled in London's Green Park. Initially, Dresden objected to the memorial but an inscription commemorating all the lives lost during the bombing raids eased their concerns.

Bomber Command Memorial, Green Park, London.
Photographed by the author.

In December 2012, British Prime Minister, David Cameron, acknowledged that the veterans of Bomber Command had 'been treated inconsistently with those who served in Fighter Command'.

28 April 1945
The Execution of Mussolini

On 28 April 1945, Benito Mussolini and his mistress, Clara Petacci, were executed by partisans as they tried to flee Italy.

1943: the war was going badly for Italy, the Allies had landed in Sicily and the future looked bleak.

On 24 July 1943, at a meeting of the Fascist Grand Council, Benito Mussolini delivered an impassioned two-hour speech, exhorting his fellow fascists to put up a fight. His plea fell on deaf ears, the Council instead voting to propose peace with the Allies.

The following day the Italian king, Victor Emmanuel III, dismissed Mussolini. Mussolini was immediately arrested and imprisoned. The Italian population rejoiced.

On 8 September, Italy swapped sides and joined the Allies. Italy's wish to remain neutral was vetoed by Churchill who demanded Italy's cooperation against the Germans as the price for the "passage back." On 13 October 1943, Italy reluctantly declared war on Germany. Immediately, the Germans started capturing Italians as prisoners of war, shipping them to internment camps and began the targeting of Italian Jews.

The daring rescue

On 12 September 1943 on Hitler's orders, Mussolini was rescued from his mountainside captivity by SS paratroopers and whisked away to Germany in a glider. Having met with Hitler, Mussolini was returned to Italy and set up as the head of a Fascist republic in German-occupied northern Italy.

But by April 1945, with the Allies advancing north through Italy, Mussolini knew the end was in sight. Together with his mistress, Clara Petacci (pictured below), and a few followers, Mussolini fled and headed for the Swiss border. Stopped by Italian partisans on 26 April, Mussolini's attempts to disguise himself with a Luftwaffe overcoat and helmet had failed.

On 28 April, at the picturesque Lake Como, the partisans stopped the car; pushed Mussolini and Petacci out, and ordered them against a wall. Whilst the partisans pronounced the death sentence, Petacci flung her arms around Mussolini and screamed, "No, he mustn't die." Petacci was shot and fell. Mussolini ripped open his jacket and screamed, 'Shoot me in the chest!' The executioner, a communist partisan by the name of Walter Audisio, did so. Mussolini fell but was not dead. Another bullet in the chest ensured that he was. The bodies were heaped into the back of a van, together with those of Mussolini's last followers, and transported to Milan.

A rusty beam

Their bodies were delivered to the Piazzale Loreto, the scene of a mass execution of partisans the year before. The corpses were beaten and urinated upon and finally left to hang upside down, for public display, from a rusty beam outside a petrol station. Petacci had not been wearing knickers and a group of old women rearranged her skirt to preserve her modesty. People surged around, desperate to get a look, to laugh and spit upon them, wanting to make sure that it was true: Mussolini, fascist dictator of Italy for twenty-three years, was truly dead and Italy could live again.

Two days later, Hitler was also dead.

30 April 1945,
The Death of Adolf Hitler

In January 1945, with the Soviet Red Army bearing down on Germany, Hitler left his HQ in East Prussia and moved back to Berlin and into the Reich Chancellery. A month later, he went underground into the Chancellery's air-raid shelter, a cavern of dimly-lit rooms made of solid, high-quality concrete.

Hitler's Health

During his last few months, Hitler's health deteriorated rapidly. In February 1945, after so many years of shouting and screaming, he had to have an operation on his vocal chords which obliged him to stay silent for a whole week.

Despite the implorations of his staff, Hitler refused to leave Berlin, and finally, realising the war was truly lost, he decided to end his life. Shuffling around with a stoop, Hitler looked much older than his fifty-six years. A new pain in his eye required daily doses of cocaine drops, and, perhaps from the onset of Parkinson's disease, his left hand shook constantly. His eyesight had become so poor

169

he had to have his documents written in extra-large print on specially-made 'Fuhrer' typewriters.

Adolf Hitler, 1938. German Federal Archive.

He ate poorly – devouring large portions of cake. He'd fallen out with many of his senior colleagues – in particular Hermann Goring and Heinrich Himmler, both of whom he accused of treachery and ordered to be arrested on sight and court-martialled. Joseph Goebbels, however, remained loyal to the last, broadcasting to the nation, demanding greater effort and sacrifice against the enemy.

Hitler the General

In his final days Hitler ordered a scorched-earth policy throughout eastern Germany and the destruction of anything that could be of use to the Soviets. What happened to the German citizen was not of Hitler's concern – as far as he was concerned, they had proved themselves unworthy of him.

From within the bunker, Hitler continued to dictate operations but his grip on reality had deserted him. He refused to listen to the glum reports from the front and ordered a constant stream of counterattacks deploying non-existent troops and refusing the troops that did exist room to retreat and re-group.

On his fifty-sixth (and last) birthday on 20 April 1945, a group of nineteen or so Hitler Youth boys lined-up in the Chancellery garden for Hitler to inspect and decorate with Iron Crosses. Lined-up from the eldest to the youngest, Hitler, with his shaking left hand behind his back, shook hands with each child, pinching the cheek of the last, the youngest child, a twelve-year-old boy called Alfred Czech. 'The Führer shook my hand,' said Mr Czech decades later, 'then he pinched my left cheek. He told me, "Keep it up!" I certainly had the feeling that I had done something remarkable.' Hitler delivered a short speech and thanked them for their bravery before shuffling back into the bunker. It was to be Hitler's last appearance in public.

Eva Braun, June 1942. German Federal Archive.

Hitler and Eva

A week later, just past midnight on 29 April, in a ten-minute ceremony, Hitler married his long-term partner, Eva Braun. Twenty-three years his junior, the German people knew nothing of her. Her presence, although not a secret amongst the Nazi hierarchy, was not something Hitler wished publicized lest it should diminish the adoration of Germany's women. Goebbels and Martin Bormann stood as witnesses as a hastily-found registrar nervously asked the couple whether they were of pure Aryan descent and free of hereditary diseases.

That night, following the subdued and rather surreal marital celebrations, Hitler dictated his last political testament and private will to his secretary, where, in the former, he drew-up the make-up of the government following his death. The admiral, Karl Donitz, was named as his successor, not as 'Fuhrer' but as president, and Goebbels as Chancellor.

Fighting to his last breath against Bolshevism

On 29 April, Hitler made preparations for his death. Two hundred litres of benzene were delivered into the bunker. Hitler insisted that his body be burnt, not wanting his corpse to finish up in Soviet hands like an 'exhibit in a cabinet of curiosities'. He also ordered the testing of the newly-arrived batch of cyanide capsules. The chosen victim was Hitler's much-loved Alsatian dog, Blondi.

On 30 April, with the Soviets only three hundred metres away, Goebbels tried one last time to convince the Fuhrer to leave Berlin but Hitler had already made it plain a week earlier, bellowing at his generals, 'If you gentlemen think I'm going to leave Berlin you are very much mistaken. I'd rather blow my brains out'.

Near four o'clock on the 30th, after a round of farewells, Hitler and his wife of forty hours retired to his study. Hitler wore upon his tunic, his Iron Cross (First Class) and his Wounded Badge of the First World War. His entourage waited anxiously outside. A shot was heard. Hitler had shot himself through the right temple. Braun was also dead. She had swallowed the cyanide. The pistol Hitler had used was the same one that his niece, Geli

Raubal, had used when she committed suicide almost fourteen years before. Hitler's body, collapsing over the table, overturned a vase, the water it contained drenching Eva's top.

U.S. Army newspaper Stars and Stripes *announcing Hitler's death, May 1945.*

The bodies, covered in blankets, were carried out into the Chancellery garden. There, with artillery exploding around them and neighbouring buildings ablaze, Hitler's wishes were honoured – the benzene was poured on the corpses and set alight. With the bodies blazing, the entourage gave one final Hitler salute before scampering back into the bunker.

The official announcement, the following day, stated that 'Hitler had fallen at his command post fighting to his last breath against Bolshevism and for Germany'.

Hitler had come to power as German Chancellor, aged forty-three, in January 1933. But with his death, the Third Reich, which was meant to last a thousand years, had come to an end after just twelve.

24 October 1945
The Execution of Vidkun Quisling

On 24 October 1945, Vidkun Quisling, the Norwegian Nazi, was executed as the ultimate traitor, and a new word entered common usage.

Born 18 July 1887, Vidkun Quisling's life and early career had started promisingly. As a child, the son of a Lutheran pastor, he was considered somewhat a mathematical child prodigy and, as a young cadet coming out of military school, he gained the highest recorded marks in Norway.

Vidkun Quisling, CBE

After leaving the army, where he had worked his way up to the rank of Major, Quisling worked as a humanitarian, helping with the great famines in Russia during the 1920s. It was in Russia he became an avid anti-Communist and, in doing so, helped British interests in their diplomatic wrangling with the Soviets. In 1929 the British, so grateful to Quisling for his help, awarded him the CBE.

Between 1931 and 1933 Quisling was Norway's Minister of Defence but then, disillusioned with democracy, resigned and formed his own 'National Unity' party, a Norwegian equivalent of the German Nazi Party. But the Norwegians had little time for fascism and in the 1933 national elections, Quisling's party polled little more than two percent of the vote and gained no seats.

Quisling and Hitler

With no support and no influence, Quisling looked destined to wither away into obscurity. But in Adolf Hitler, whom Quisling visited in December 1939, he had a friend.

In April 1940, Quisling met German agents in Copenhagen and divulged secrets concerning Norway's defences. Six days later – Germany invaded. On 9 April, Quisling stormed into the studios of Oslo's radio station and declared himself prime minister. German representatives demanded that Norway's king, Haakon VII, recognise Quisling. The king refused but, in danger, went into exile to England and there formed a government-in-exile.

With German backing, Quisling ordered all resistance to stop. Once Germany had established control of Norway the Nazis put Quisling in charge of their government of occupation. So trusting were the Germans of their Norwegian puppet that two years later, in 1942, they appointed Quisling Prime Minister and granted him full license to run the country without interference.

But on 9 May 1945, the day after Germany's unconditional surrender, Quisling was arrested. King Haakon returned to his country, arriving amidst emotional scenes of jubilation.

Norway had abolished capital punishment in 1905, but its government-in-exile reinstated it specifically for Quisling and his highest-ranking colleagues. Hence, charged with high treason, Quisling was executed by firing squad on 24 October 1945. He was fifty-eight.

The Definition of Quisling

The word *quisling* entered common usage during the war as a term denoting a traitor. Today, in the Oxford English Dictionary, a quisling is defined as, 'a person cooperating with an occupying enemy force; a collaborator; a traitor.'

23 December 1948
The Execution of Hideki Tojo

On 23 December 1948, former prime minister of Japan, Hideki Tojo, was executed for war crimes.

Born in Tokyo on 30 December 1884, Hideki Tojo, the son of a general, was brought up in a military environment that held little regard for politicians or civilians. An admirer of Adolf Hitler, Tojo advocated closer ties between Japan and Germany and Italy, and in September 1940, the three Axis powers signed the Tripartite Pact.

Appointed Japan's Minister for War in July 1940, Tojo was keen to accelerate the coming war against the US. He viewed the US as a weak nation, populated by degenerate and lazy civilians. Tojo was appointed Japan's prime minister in October 1941 and within two months had ordered the attack on Pearl Harbor, thus turning the war into a global conflict.

As well as prime minister and minister for war, Hideki Tojo was also appointed home and foreign minister. From February 1944 he was also made Commander-in-Chief of the General Staff. Thus, he ruled almost as dictator, answerable only to Emperor Hirohito.

But as the war turned against Japan, Tojo faced mounting pressure from his government and military hierarchy. Eventually, on 18 July 1944, after a string of losses, the Emperor obliged Tojo to resign.

Following the atomic bombs over Hiroshima and Nagasaki in early August 1945, Tojo was amongst those who maintained Japan should still not surrender.

Hideki Tojo, c1945.

Sorry it is taking me so long to die

In September 1945, following Japan's surrender, Tojo tried to resist capture by the Americans by committing suicide – shooting himself in the heart. With US military police pounding at the door of his Tokyo home, his doctor used a piece of charcoal to draw a circle on Tojo's chest, pinpointing the exact location where Tojo should aim. However, Tojo somehow missed, shooting himself in the stomach. 'I am very sorry it is taking me so long to die', he mumbled as he was arrested. 'I await for the righteous judgment of history. I wished to commit suicide but sometimes that fails.' Nationalists were appalled that Tojo, having advocated suicide to his countrymen, had failed to take his own life. His use of a gun was considered cowardly – it should have been a samurai sword.

Having survived his suicide attempt, Tojo was placed in prison. While incarcerated, an American dentist set him up with a new set of dentures. Unbeknownst to Tojo, the dentist had secretly drilled his teeth with the words 'Remember Pearl Harbor', written in Morse Code.

Having been nursed back to health, Tojo was tried as a war criminal and found guilty. He went out of his way to take responsibility, deflecting all blame from the emperor. At his trial, he declared, 'It is natural that I should bear entire responsibility for the war in general, and, needless to say, I am prepared to do so.'

Along with six other 'Class A' war criminals, Hideki Tojo, a week shy of his sixty-fourth birthday, was executed by hanging at Sugamo Prison on 23 December 1948.

In August 2015, on the seventieth anniversary of Japan's defeat, a Chinese ice cream manufacturer celebrated the occasion by selling ice creams depicting Tojo's face.

Images and Disclaimers

All the images used in this book are, as far as I can ascertain, in the public domain. If I have mistakenly used an image that is not in the public domain, please let me know at felix@historyinanhour.com and I shall remove / replace the offending item as soon as I can.

Also, while I have taken great care to ensure every fact and figure is correct, there are a lot of them and I am only human. Therefore, if you spot a mistake, please just let me know without exposing me too publicly, and I will check and amend if necessary. Thank you.

Complete Series:

The Clever Teens' Guide to World War One
The Clever Teens' Guide to World War Two
The Clever Teens' Guide to the Russian Revolution
The Clever Teens' Guide to Nazi Germany
The Clever Teens' Guide to the Cold War

The Clever Teens' Tales From World War One
The Clever Teens' Tales From World War Two
The Clever Teens' Tales From the Cold War

Printed in Great Britain
by Amazon

62446933R00113